everyday
HANDMADE

22 practical projects for the modern sewist

Cassie Barden and Adrienne Smitke

dedication

To my partner and best friend, Jon, who provides me endless support, encouragement, insightful creative input, and sound advice every day. It means so much that you truly believe in me, and my life is richer and more creative with you in it!

~ Cassie

To my family, who have supported and encouraged all of my creative endeavors: my amazing and talented mom, who taught me to sew, my devoted dad for being my #1 fan, and my wonderful and creative sister, who is always available for a design consultation. I'm so lucky to have all of you.

~ Adrienne

Everyday Handmade: 22 Practical Projects for the Modern Sewist © 2011 by Cassie Barden and Adrienne Smitke

That Patchwork Place® is an imprint of Martingale & Company®.

Martingale & Company
19021 120th Ave. NE, Suite 102
Bothell, WA 98011
www.martingale-pub.com

Printed in China
16 15 14 13 12 11   8 7 6 5 4 3 2 1

Library of Congress Cataloging-in-Publication Data is available upon request.

ISBN: 978-1-60468-052-2

credits

President & CEO: Tom Wierzbicki
Editor in Chief: Mary V. Green
Managing Editor: Karen Costello Soltys
Technical Editor: Christine Barnes
Copy Editor: Melissa Bryan
Design Director: Stan Green
Production Manager: Regina Girard
Illustrator: Laurel Strand
Cover & Text Designer: Shelly Garrison
Photographer: Brent Kane

mission statement

Dedicated to providing quality products and service to inspire creativity.

CONTENTS

HANDMADE
is awesome

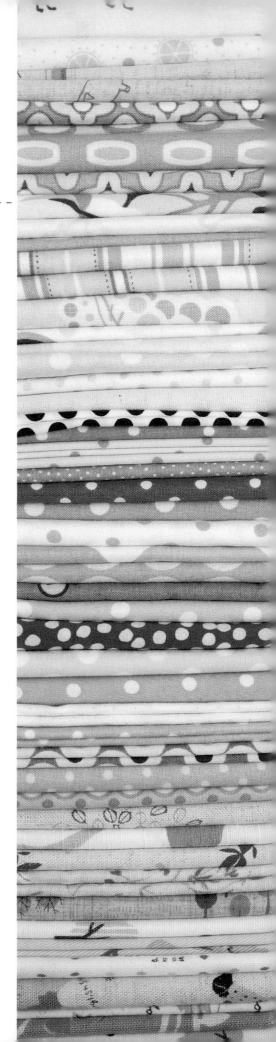

Handmade *IS* awesome. It sounds silly, but it's true! For us, making things by hand is fun, creative, and deeply satisfying. We're the type of people who constantly have an in-progress project (or two, or three) and who relish the idea of making Christmas and birthday gifts by hand for the special people in our lives. We live in an area with a thriving and supportive craft community, and we're excited to be able to contribute to it.

Although we met as coworkers, we soon discovered that we had many things in common, including our love of sewing. We both came from creative households where *doing-it-yourself* was always encouraged. Both our moms taught us to sew when we were young, and despite going on to explore other creative avenues, we each came back to sewing because it combined our love for design, color, texture, and making things by hand.

We believe handmade objects can be practical *and* beautiful. In this book you'll find more than 20 projects that you'll not only enjoy sewing, but also enjoy using every day. To help you personalize your projects, we've included our favorite approaches to appliqué, embroidery, and other embellishments, such as covered buttons and yo-yos. In addition, you'll get sewing and quilting basics, plus tips on choosing the perfect fabric, essential tools, and how to make the most of each project.

While you need only basic sewing skills to get started on the easier projects, there are plenty of patterns to inspire and challenge more experienced sewists. Beginners looking for a place to start should read through "General Instructions" beginning on page 101, but don't be afraid to dive right in.

We're in the midst of a handmade revival, and more and more people are discovering the satisfaction of creating things by hand. In her first book, *The New Handmade* (Martingale & Company, 2008), Cassie wrote, "When you hand-make something, you recognize the value of the process, of your unique vision, of your creativity. You imbue the handmade with a bit of yourself—a gift that you've made by hand is a very special gift indeed." This statement resonates with both of us, and we hope the projects in this book spark your creativity, inspire self-expression, and give you the joy of being able to say, "I made this."

~ Cassie & Adrienne

Fabric options for the modern sewist are vast indeed. From simple quilting cottons to designer home-decor weights to organic hemp or ripstop nylon, there is something out there that is perfect for your project. We tend to use a few kinds of fabric over and over in our projects, but as with everything in this book, experimentation is encouraged!

quilting cottons

The mainstay of modern sewists everywhere, quilting cottons are widely available in independent quilt shops and through full-service fabric stores, online sites, and chain retailers. Avoid cottons that feel scratchy, stiff, or have an obvious weave; they are likely of lower quality and won't wear as nicely.

medium-weight cottons and linen

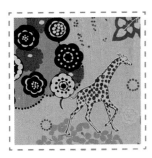

The past few years have seen an explosion of medium-weight cottons by big-name designers, and with good reason. More structured than quilting cotton but without the heavy bulk of upholstery fabric, medium-weight cotton is perfect for bags and home accessories. The influx of Japanese fabrics has popularized 100% linen and cotton-linen blends. The blends can be a bit heavier than quilting cottons but retain a lovely texture. You'll find that 100% linen is airy and natural, and makes a gorgeous neutral background for patchwork and embroidery.

felt

Most felt is made from wool, a wool-rayon blend, or acrylic. Manufactured in different thicknesses, 1 mm is the standard choice for most felt projects, but 2 mm and thicker is available. Avoid the sheets of scratchy, thin "craft felt"—it's the most readily available but also of the poorest quality. Felt of 100% wool, available as yardage or in sheets, is gorgeous and comes in a wide variety of shades, including one-of-a-kind hand-dyed colors. In addition, many high-quality felts are wool-rayon blends, and in fact our personal favorite is a blend from Japan. See "Online Resources" (page 110).

nylon, oilcloth, laminates

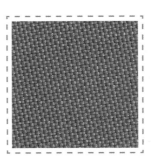

A less common but very useful fabric for bags is ripstop nylon, found in larger fabric stores and stores specializing in outdoor fabrics. Ripstop nylon is thin and easy to work with, and it's also very sturdy. It comes in a variety of solid colors and makes a great lining for any bag that will get heavy use.

Other fabrics to experiment with are oilcloth and vinyl-coated cotton, also known as laminate. Oilcloth is heavier and the prints tend toward kitsch, while laminates are lighter and available in many current designs. Both are sturdy and easy to wipe clean.

upcycled fabrics

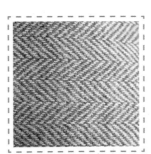

Although it's terribly difficult to resist crisp new cottons, with a little creativity you can find textiles for your projects anywhere. Old dress shirts, tweed suits, worn leather, and felted wool sweaters can all find new life as a bag, stuffed animal, or e-reader sleeve.

fabric resources

With all the amazing prints and designer fabrics coming out every season, hunting down the perfect fabric is half the fun of sewing. Although we are often asked where we find our fabric, we hope you won't get too caught up in trying to track down the exact fabrics we used in the book. Choosing your own fabric is a great way to personalize a project and make it your own. Here are some ideas for where to start shopping.

Local quilt/fabric shops. The big chain stores might carry more bolts of fabric, but smaller, independent shops often specialize in certain fabric styles or contemporary designers, and shopping locally supports the creative community where you live. Get acquainted with the shops in your area, and you'll know just where to look when searching for that perfect batik or the newest line from your favorite designer.

Online. With the wealth of online fabric retailers popping up over the last few years, the Internet is one of the best places to find the latest and most unusual fabrics. But there's so much out there, it can be overwhelming. If you're looking for something specific, search using multiple descriptive keywords to narrow down your results. One of our favorite online sites for fabric shopping is the online marketplace Etsy.com. Etsy gives you access to countless sellers through one search engine. Quilting cottons and sewing notions are sold side by side with one-of-a-kind and hard-to-find fabrics from around the world.

Thrift stores. Want your sewing to have vintage flair and be environmentally friendly? Try checking your local thrift shops for clothing that can be upcycled and repurposed. In addition to vintage finds, thrift stores are a great source for wool blends, linens, and other materials that are much more expensive in traditional fabric stores.

For more ideas on where to get specific materials we used in this book, check out "Online Resources" (page 110) for a listing of some of our favorite shops.

preparing your fabric

There are no hard-and-fast rules for prewashing. Generally, we recommend prewashing anything that might get washed in the future, or that could bleed or shrink. Use your best judgment. Vintage or thrift-store fabrics will probably need to be washed to get rid of odors or test for colorfastness, but if you don't know the fiber content, stick to hand washing to avoid shrinking or ruining the fabric. Once washed and dried, fabric from recycled clothing should be cut apart at the seams and all linings, buttons, and other notions (like zippers) removed.

Before starting any project, make sure your fabric is flat and free of major creases or wrinkles. Iron using the steam setting and the appropriate temperature for the fabric.

Cassie's Tips for Small-Space Sewing

While working on this book I lived in a teensy-tiny apartment less than 400 square feet, and my "sewing studio" was also my bedroom. If you're struggling to work effectively in a tiny space, here are some things I've learned from experience.

- Keep it tidy. Putting everything away after one task means you can start the next one when inspiration stikes—not after cleaning up the last one.

- Storage can be a big challenge in a tiny space, but don't let clutter accumulate just because too many things lack homes. Use hooks, wall shelves, and under-the-bed storage to your advantage.

- I used an insulated ironing pad for years, but it's hardly ideal for larger pieces of fabric. A better option is to install a full-sized ironing board that folds down from the wall or hangs from a door.

- A design wall is a great tool that allows you to stand back and see your project as you go. Try creating your own design surface by tacking a large piece of batting to an empty wall. In lieu of wall space, lay a large piece of batting on your bed. Stand on a chair to get a better view. When you're done for the day, roll up your batting—and your project—until next time.

- If possible, choose paint colors and furniture to create an environment that's light and airy. Use full-spectrum bulbs to mimic daylight. A well-lit sewing space—even a tiny one—will be motivating, inspiring, and fun to work in.

collector's item TOTE BAG

Use your favorite fabrics to make the custom-covered buttons that decorate this simple shopper-style tote. The embroidered grid creates the perfect canvas for showing off your collection. You could also display a selection of antique buttons, 1" pins, or charms. Best of all, once you're finished sewing, this tote is the perfect size to take to the fabric store or the flea market when shopping for additions to your favorite collection.

Designed and sewn by
Adrienne Smitke

Finished Size: 12" x 14½" x 2½"

materials

Yardage is based on 42"-wide fabric.

1 yard of natural linen for bag exterior

1 yard of dark pink polka-dot cotton fabric for lining and straps

2 yards of 20"-wide medium-weight fusible interfacing

20 scraps, at least 3" x 3", of assorted fabrics to cover buttons

20 metal button forms, 1⅛" diameter*

White embroidery floss

Embroidery hoop (optional)

*I used Dritz button forms, which come with a tool for applying the fabric.

cutting

From the natural linen, cut:
1 rectangle, 14" x 16½"
1 rectangle, 13" x 15½"
2 rectangles, 3½" x 15½"
1 rectangle, 3½" x 13"

From the polka-dot fabric, cut:
2 rectangles, 13" x 15½"
2 rectangles, 3½" x 15½"
1 rectangle, 3½" x 13"
2 strips, 6" x 24"

From the interfacing, cut:
4 rectangles, 13" x 15½"
4 rectangles, 3½" x 15½"
2 rectangles, 3½" x 13"

embroidering the bag

Use ½" seam allowances.

1. With the marking tool of your choice, draw a 7" x 8¾" rectangle centered on the 14" x 16½" linen rectangle. Divide the rectangle into five rows of 1¾" x 1¾" squares, with four squares in each row. ❶

2. Referring to "Embroidery" (page 106), use three strands of white embroidery floss and a running stitch to stitch the marked lines. If you prefer, use an embroidery hoop to hold the fabric taut while stitching. Take short, even stitches and tie a knot to secure the loose ends on the back of the fabric. ❷

3. Trim the embroidered linen rectangle to 13" x 15½", positioning the grid as shown. ❸

making the bag

1. Following the manufacturer's instructions, fuse a 13" x 15½" piece of medium-weight interfacing to the wrong side of the embroidered linen square. Repeat with the remaining bag exterior and lining pieces and their corresponding interfacing pieces.

2. With right sides together, stitch a 3½" x 15½" linen rectangle to each long edge of the embroidered rectangle. Stop stitching ½" before the bottom edge, backstitching at the beginning and end of each seam. Press the seam allowances open. Stitch the remaining 13" x 15½" linen rectangle to either edge of the unit. ❹

3. Join the remaining lengthwise edges to create a tube, again stopping ½" before the bottom edge. Press the seam allowances open. ❺

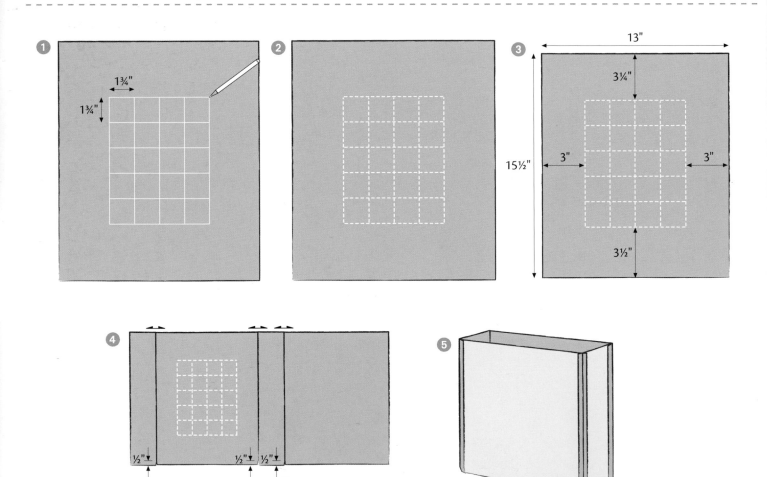

4. With right sides together, pin the 3½" x 13" linen rectangle to the bottom of the tube. Fold the corners up 90° so that the bag sits flat. **6**

5. Starting in the middle of one long side, stitch around the bottom of the bag. Pivot at each corner, stitch across the point, and backstitch. Trim the corners, making sure not to cut too close to the seam. Turn the bag right side out. **7**

6. Repeat steps 2 and 3 with the lining fabric, leaving a 6" gap along one side seam and backstitching at either end of the gap. Repeat steps 4 and 5, but do not turn the lining right side out.

7. Following the manufacturer's instructions, cover the 20 metal button forms with assorted scraps. Generally, medium-weight fabric or quilting cotton works best. Arrange the buttons on the stitched grid, centering each button in a square. When you are happy with the placement, hand sew the buttons to the bag with white embroidery floss, knotting the tails on the back of the fabric.

Metal button forms for covering are available at your local crafts or fabric store.

8. To make the straps, fold a 6" x 24" polka-dot strip in half *lengthwise*, wrong sides together, and press. Open the strip and turn the raw edges in to meet the fold. Refold, enclosing the raw edges, and press. Topstitch a scant ⅛" from each edge. Make two straps. **8**

Covered-Button Tip

If you're using thin or gauzy fabrics, fuse a piece of *lightweight* interfacing to the back of the scrap to keep the metal from showing through on the front of the button.

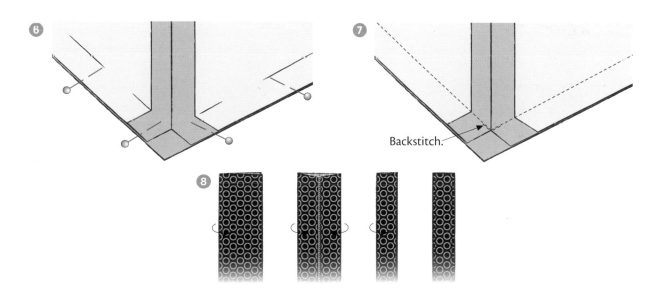

Backstitch.

assembling the bag

1. Pin the straps 1½" from either edge on both the front and back of the bag exterior.

2. With right sides together, slip the bag exterior inside the bag lining, sandwiching the straps between the layers. Align and pin or clip (with metal hairclips) the edges together. Sew around the top of the bag, backstitching over the seams and straps. **9**

3. Turn right side out by pulling the entire bag through the gap in the lining seam. Refer to "Finishing Stitches" (page 106) and use the stitch of your choice to close the gap. **10**

4. Push the lining inside the bag exterior, roll the top seam (page 104), and press the bag. Topstitch ¼" from the upper edge.

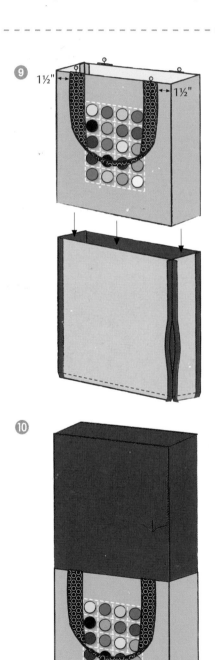

garden party selvage
WRISTLET

Selvages are the finished edges of woven fabric, often printed with the names of the fabric company, the designer, and those characteristic color-registration dots. Selvages used to be discarded without a second thought, but this sweet wristlet is the perfect reason to start your own selvage collection, and it's just the right size for your essentials. Dress it up with flower yo-yos and buttons or personalize it with other embellishments.

Designed and sewn by
Adrienne Smitke

Finished Size: 9½" x 5¼"

materials

Yardage is based on 42"-wide fabric.

Approximately 10½ yards of printed selvage strips in various lengths (see "Preparing Selvage Strips," page 15)

¼ yard of muslin

One fat quarter of green tone-on-tone fabric for trim and strap

One fat quarter of pink-and-green floral fabric for lining

4" x 4" square *each* of pink and red fabric for yo-yos

¼ yard of 20"-wide lightweight fusible interfacing

9" zipper

1½" swivel clip (see "Bag Hardware," page 32)

Two decorative buttons, approximately 11 mm (⁷⁄₁₆") diameter

cutting

From the muslin, cut:
4 rectangles, 6" x 5½"

From the green tone-on-tone fabric, cut:
2 strips, 1¾" x 10½"
1 strip, 1½" x 17½"; cut into:
　　1 strip, 1½" x 15"
　　1 rectangle, 1½" x 2½"

From the pink-and-green floral, cut:
2 rectangles, 10½" x 6"

From the interfacing, cut:
2 strips, 1¾" x 10½"

From the pink and red squares, cut:
One circle, 4" diameter
One circle, 3" diameter

Preparing Selvage Strips

So many yards of selvages can seem like an overwhelming quantity of fabric, especially because you'll want to use mostly strips with printing. Here are some tips to help gather your selvages.

• When you trim selvages off yardage, remember to leave ¼" for a seam allowance beyond the selvage edge.

• Have a special bag to collect the selvages. Each time you start a new project, trim the selvages off your yardage and put them in the bag.

• Next time you go on a sewing or quilting retreat, let your friends know you're collecting selvages and have them save theirs for you.

making the wristlet body

Use ½" seam allowances unless otherwise indicated.

1. With a muslin rectangle positioned as shown, use an acrylic ruler and a marking tool to draw a 45° line approximately ¾" from the lower-left corner. **1**

2. Lay a selvage strip slightly longer than the drawn line across the corner, right side up, aligning the raw edge of the strip with the line. Lay a second, slightly longer strip on top of the first strip so that its finished edge overlaps the raw seam allowance of the strip underneath. Stitch through all three layers—both selvage strips and the muslin—staying as close as possible to the finished edge of the top strip. Press the seam flat. **2**

3. Continue to overlap and stitch the selvage strips one at a time, stacking them like shingles and working your way up and across until the entire rectangle is covered. Make two rectangles and two rectangles reversed. Trim the rectangles to 5¾" x 5¼". **3**

4. Pair one regular and one reversed selvage rectangle to create a chevron pattern. With right sides together, pin the rectangles along the center edge. Stitch. Press the seam allowances open. Repeat to make a second unit.

5. Using the corner template on page 17, mark and trim the bottom corners on the wrong side of each rectangle.

6. Following the manufacturer's instructions, fuse the lightweight interfacing to the wrong side of each 1¾" x 10½" green tone-on-tone strip.

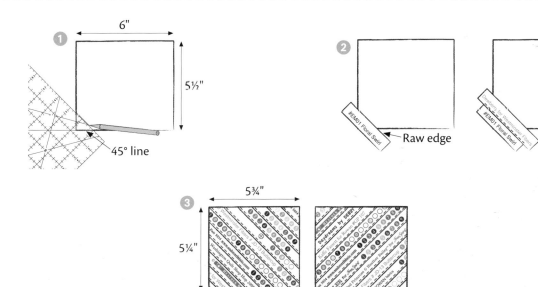

Make 2 and 2 reversed.

Simplified Wristlet

Don't have a collection of selvages, but can't wait to try this pattern? You can substitute a fat quarter of a medium-weight print and ½ yard of lightweight fusible interfacing. From each, cut two rectangles, 10½" x 5¼".

Fuse the interfacing to the wrong sides of the print rectangles. Use the corner template on page 17 to mark and trim the bottom corners. Continue with step 6 (page 15).

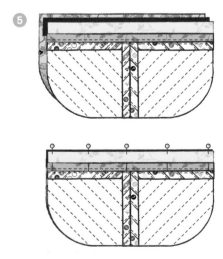

7. With right sides together, sew a green strip to the top of each selvage set. Press the seam allowances open. Topstitch a scant ⅛" on either side of the seam. Make two. ④

8. Use the template to mark and trim the bottom corners of each pink-and-green lining rectangle.

installing the zipper

1. Align the zipper, right side up, along the top edge of a pink-and-green lining piece, also right side up. Align a selvage unit, *wrong side up*, over the zipper and the lining. Pin. ⑤

2. Using a zipper foot and a ¼" seam allowance, sew through all layers, backstitching at the beginning and end. Move the zipper pull as needed to make stitching along the zipper easier. Press the fabrics away from the zipper using low heat and the point of your iron.

3. Repeat steps 1 and 2 with the remaining lining piece and selvage unit on the opposite side of the zipper.

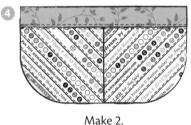

Make 2.

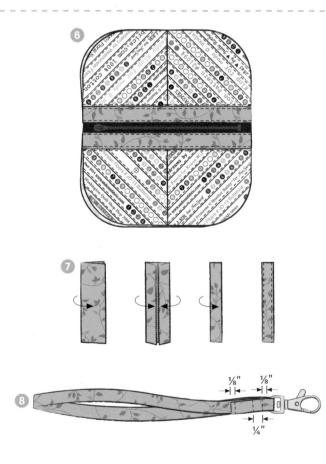

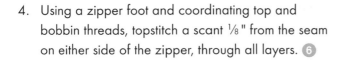

4. Using a zipper foot and coordinating top and bobbin threads, topstitch a scant ⅛" from the seam on either side of the zipper, through all layers. **6**

assembling the wristlet

1. To make the tab, fold the 1½" x 2½" green tone-on-tone rectangle in half lengthwise, wrong sides together, and press. Open the rectangle and turn the raw edges in to meet the fold. Refold, enclosing the raw edges, and press. Topstitch the length of the tab on both sides, ⅛" from the edges. **7**

2. Fold the tab in half to make a loop and baste ¼" from the raw ends.

3. To make the strap, turn ½" at one end of the 1½" x 15" green tone-on-tone strip to the wrong side and press. Repeat step 1 to finish the strap.

4. Slide the strap through the end of the swivel clip. Bring the ends together to make a loop and overlap the finished end 1", next to the swivel clip. Using your zipper foot, stitch through all three layers of the strap as shown. Set the strap aside. **8**

5. Unzip the zipper halfway. (You'll turn the bag right side out through the open zipper, so don't forget this step!) Bring the outer pieces right sides together and the lining pieces right sides together, matching the raw edges and letting the zipper tape fold over on itself at each end, with the zipper teeth toward the outer fabric, not the lining. (The zipper teeth will face upward once the finished bag is turned right side out.)

6. Slip the tab between the two bag exterior pieces, just below the seam joining the selvages and the green tone-on-tone trim. Align the raw edges and pin.

7. Starting along the bottom edge of the lining, sew around the perimeter of the entire piece, leaving a 4" gap in the lining for turning. **9**

8. Pull the bag right side out through the gap in the lining and the open zipper. Refer to "Finishing Stitches" (page 106) to close the gap. Push the lining inside the bag and clip the swivel hook through the tab on the side of the bag.

9. To make a yo-yo, turn ¼" to the wrong side of the red or pink circle. Use a loose running stitch to sew around the circle, through the seam allowance. Pull the threads tight to gather the yo-yo, and then take a few stitches to secure. Hand stitch the yo-yo and a decorative button to the front of the bag. Repeat to make and attach the second yo-yo. **10**

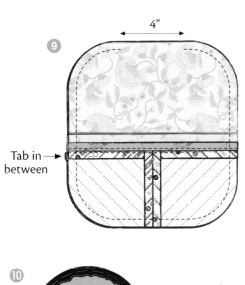

Tab in between

4"

9

10

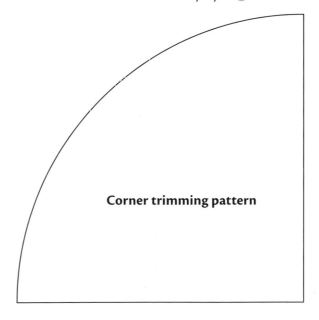

Corner trimming pattern

the portlander
SHOULDER BAG

This classic shoulder bag is the perfect size for everyday use. Whether you're headed to work or off to the farmers' market, fill it with all your essentials. The interior pockets are sized to hold a cell phone and an iPod. A sturdy but stylish medium-weight fabric and interfaced handles will make this a year-round accessory.

Designed and sewn by
Adrienne Smitke

Finished Size: 14" (at the widest point) x 12½" (not including straps)

materials

Yardage is based on 42"-wide fabric, except where indicated.

½ yard of 54"-wide brown print home-decor fabric for bag exterior

½ yard of 54"-wide natural linen for yokes and handles

⅝ yard of gray-and-yellow polka-dot fabric for lining and pockets

⅛ yard of blue solid for trim

1⅞ yards of 20"-wide medium-weight fusible interfacing

Painter's tape or removable fabric marker

4" x 4" scrap of pink-and-red polka-dot fabric to cover button

Metal button form, 2⅛" diameter

Magnetic clasp

cutting

From the brown print, cut:
2 rectangles, 16" x 12"

From the linen, cut:
4 strips, 4½" x 14"
2 strips, 6" x 20"

From the blue solid, cut:
2 strips, 1½" x 15"

From the gray-and-yellow polka-dot fabric, cut:
2 rectangles, 16" x 12"
1 rectangle, 9" x 13"

From the interfacing, cut:
2 rectangles, 16" x 12"
2 strips, 4½" x 14"
1 rectangle, 6½" x 9"
2 strips, 6" x 20"

making the bag exterior

Use ½" seam allowances unless otherwise indicated.

1. Using a marking tool and the corner template on page 23, trim the bottom corners of the 16" x 12" brown print rectangles. To form the pleats on the front and back of the bag, mark the top of each piece 2½" and 3½" from either edge. Bring the inner marks on top of the outer marks on either side. Pin. **1**

2. For the trim, fold the 1½" x 15" blue strips in half lengthwise, wrong sides together, and press. Pin the strips to the bag exterior pieces, aligning the top raw edges. Use a ¼" seam allowance and a long stitch to baste the strips and pleats. Trim the strips even with the sides. **2**

3. Fold two 4½" x 14" linen strips in half widthwise, right sides together. Using the yoke template on page 23, match the labeled edge of the template to the fabric fold. Mark and cut two yoke pieces.

4. With right sides together, sew a yoke piece to a bag exterior piece. Press the seam allowances open. Make two.

5. With right sides together, pin the two bag pieces around the sides and bottom, matching the yoke seams and the trim at the sides. Sew the pieces, starting at the yoke on one side and ending at the same point on the opposite side, backstitching at the beginning and end. *Leave the top of the yoke open.* Press the seam allowances open and turn the bag right side out. **3**

making the bag lining and pockets

1. Following the manufacturer's instructions, fuse the 16" x 12" interfacing rectangles to the wrong sides of the 16" x 12" gray-and-yellow polka-dot rectangles. Use the template to round the corners.

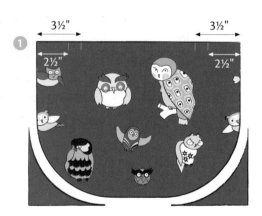

3½" 3½"
2½" 2½"

Bring inner mark to outer mark.

2. To pleat the lining, mark the top of each rectangle as you did in step 1 of "Making the Bag Exterior." However, this time bring the *outer* marks on top of the *inner* marks on either side so these pleats go in the opposite direction. Pin. Using a ¼" seam allowance, baste the top of each lining piece to secure the pleats.

3. Fuse the 4½" x 14" strips of interfacing to the two remaining 4½" x 14" linen yoke strips. Fold the strips in half and cut two yoke pieces.

Marking Seam Allowances for Accurate Sewing

I trace the seam allowances for the top edge of the yoke (shown on the template) onto the interfaced sides of the lining pieces. It's easiest to do this now, when the yoke pieces are still unsewn. Stitching on the marked lines ensures accurate seam allowances on these tight curves.

Mark the seam allowances.

4. With right sides together, sew an interfaced yoke piece to a pleated lining piece. Press the seam allowances open. Make two.

5. To make the pocket, fold the 9" x 13" gray-and-yellow polka-dot rectangle in half, right sides together, so that it measures 9" x 6½". Fuse the 6½" x 9" piece of interfacing to one side of the pocket piece. Stitch around the three open sides, leaving a 2" gap along one short side. You'll close the gap when you topstitch the pocket to the lining. 4

6. Trim the corners and turn the pocket right side out. Roll the seams (page 104) and press. Topstitch ⅛" from the folded edge.

7. Center the pocket on one of the bag lining pieces, 2" from the bottom of the yoke. Pin. Topstitch around the pocket sides and bottom a scant ⅛" from the edge, backstitching at the beginning and end. Mark the pocket with a piece of painter's tape or a removable fabric marker 3½" from one edge, and stitch to divide the pocket in two. 5

8. Just as you did with the bag exterior, pin the bag lining pieces right sides together, matching the yoke seams. Sew the pieces, starting at the top edge of the yoke on one side and ending at the same point on the opposite side, leaving a 6" gap at the bottom, and backstitching at the beginning and end of each seam. Press the seam allowances open. 6

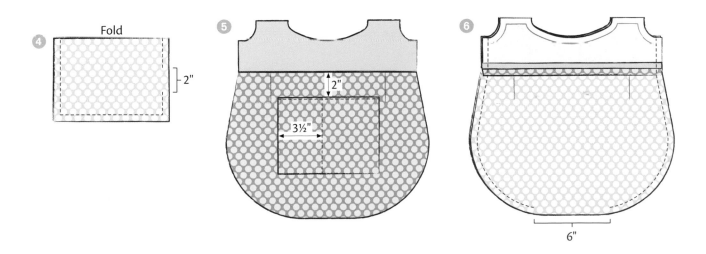

9. With the bag lining still right sides together, mark the center of each yoke 1" from the top raw edge. Working from the right side of the lining, attach each piece of the magnetic clasp so its upper edge is at the mark and the back disc is against the interfacing. (Before you install the second half of the clasp, make sure the pieces will line up.) Turn the lining right side out and press, being careful to avoid the magnetic clasp. ⑦

assembling the bag

1. To make the straps, fuse the 6" x 20" interfacing strips to the wrong side of the 6" x 20" linen strips. Fold each strip in half lengthwise, wrong sides together, and press. Open the strip and turn the raw edges in to meet the fold. Refold, enclosing the raw edges, and press. Topstitch the straps ⅛" from each long edge.

2. Pin the ends of each strap to the yoke tops on the exterior bag, aligning the raw edges. To keep the straps straight while sewing, pin them to the bag a few inches below as well. ⑧

3. With right sides together, slip the bag exterior inside the bag lining, sandwiching the straps between the two layers. Align and pin the raw edges, making sure to match the side seams. ⑨

4. Sew around the top of the bag, backstitching over the side seams and the straps. Because there are lots of tight curves, go slowly and pivot carefully. The smoother your sewing line, the better your bag will look. If you marked the seam allowances on the yoke lining, follow the lines.

5. Trim the corners at the top of the yoke where the straps are attached and clip the yoke curves every ½", being careful not to cut the stitching.

6. Turn the bag right side out by pulling it through the gap at the bottom of the lining. See "Finishing Stitches" (page 106) to close the gap. Push the lining inside the bag exterior, roll the seams (page 104), and press, being careful to avoid the magnetic clasp.

7. Topstitch the top of the bag ⅜" from the edge.

8. Cover the metal button form with the pink-and-red fabric. Hand stitch the button over the magnetic clasp on the front of the bag.

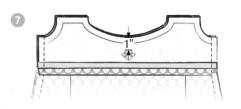

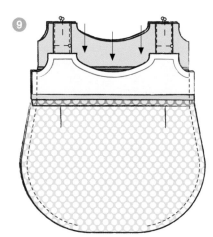

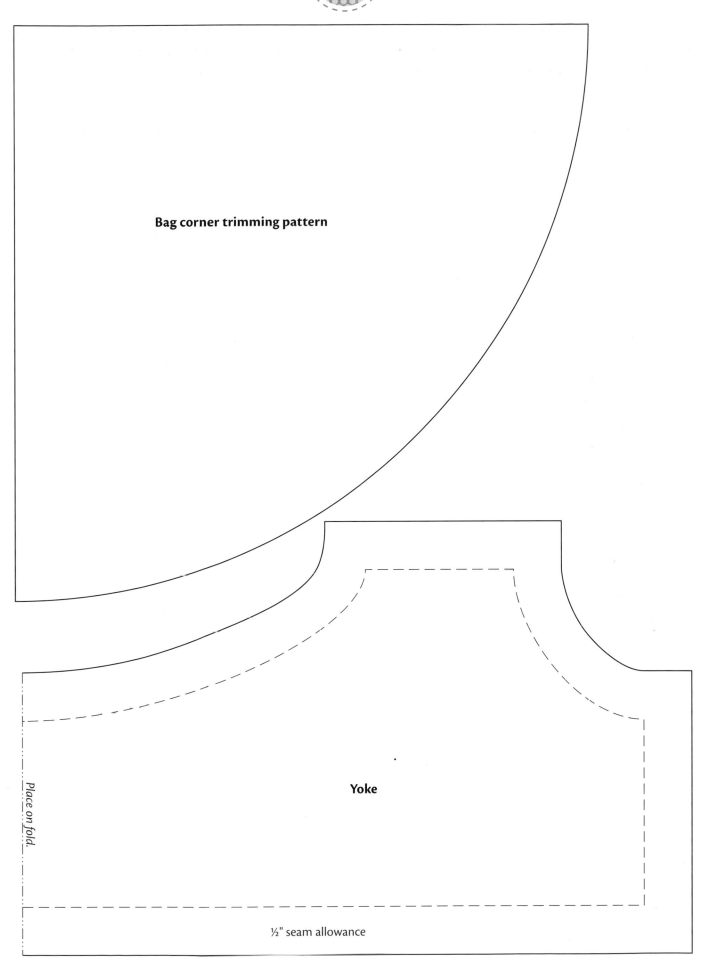

Bag corner trimming pattern

Place on fold.

Yoke

½" seam allowance

winter forest
MESSENGER BAG

Stand out in a sea of plain canvas messenger bags with this combination of gorgeous prints and hardcore utility. This is a true messenger bag, with an integrated, padded laptop sleeve, tons of pockets, and an adjustable-length shoulder strap. If you already have a laptop sleeve and don't need the extra padding, it's easy to skip that step and still have a roomy, workhorse bag to take you through work, school, and the weekend in style.

This is a long project, but the results are worth it. Just work through each section of the bag in turn, and label your pieces as you cut them to keep things organized.

Designed and sewn by
Cassie Barden

Finished Size: 16" x 12" x 4" deep; will accommodate a laptop up to 15"

materials

Yardage is based on 42"-wide fabric.

1 yard of large-scale blue-and-red cotton print for main bag and flap

⅝ yard of maroon cotton print for lining of front pocket unit

½ yard of smaller-scale blue cotton print for front pocket unit

⅓ yard of red Cordura nylon or canvas for bag bottom

2⅝ yards of gray ripstop nylon for bag lining and laptop sleeve

1⅞ yards of 20"-wide medium-weight fusible interfacing

20" sport zipper

½ yard of closed-cell foam (see "Online Resources," page 110)

1½ yards of 2"-wide black nylon webbing for shoulder strap

1⅛ yards of 1"-wide black nylon webbing for flap closure

Two 1" side-release buckles (see "Bag Hardware," page 32)

Two standard loops

One 2" single-bar slide

⅞" swivel hook

cutting for the outer bag

From the large-scale blue-and-red cotton print, cut:
4 rectangles, 3" x 11½" (side pieces H1–H4)
1 rectangle, 17" x 11½" (back piece F)
1 rectangle, 17" x 17" (back pocket piece G)
1 rectangle, 17" x 15" (outer flap)

From the blue cotton print, cut:
1 rectangle, 17" x 3" (front piece A)
2 rectangles, 6½" x 8½" (front pieces B and D)
1 rectangle, 6" x 8½" (front piece C)
1 rectangle, 6" x 11" (front piece E)

From the maroon cotton print, cut:

1 strip, 2" x 17" (back pocket binding)

1 strip, 2" x 6" (front pocket binding)

1 rectangle, 17" x 3" (front pocket lining A1/top)

1 rectangle, 17" x 8½" (front pocket lining A2/bottom)

1 rectangle, 17" x 11½" (front pocket lining A3/back)

From the red nylon or canvas, cut:

2 strips, 21" x 4½" (pieces J and K)

From the gray ripstop nylon, cut:

1 rectangle, 17" x 15" (outer flap lining)

From the interfacing, cut:

4 rectangles, 3" x 11½" (side panels H1–H4)

1 rectangle, 17" x 17" (back pocket G)

1 rectangle, 17" x 3" (front unit A)

2 rectangles, 6½" x 8½" (front units B and D)

1 rectangle, 6" x 8½" (front unit C)

1 rectangle, 6" x 11" (front pocket E)

1 rectangle, 17" x 15" (outer flap)

constructing the outer bag

Use ½" seam allowances unless otherwise indicated.

1. Fold piece E in half widthwise, wrong sides together, to make a piece 6" x 5½" and press.

2. To prepare the binding strip, fold the 2" x 6" maroon print strip in half lengthwise, wrong sides together, and press. Open the strip and turn the raw edges in to meet the fold. Refold, enclosing the raw edges, and press. Sandwich this binding strip over the folded edge of piece E and topstitch. ❶

3. Layer piece E on piece C, right sides up and raw edges aligned. With right sides together, sew pieces B and D to the sides of the unit. Press the seam allowances outward. ❷

4. Place this finished front unit right side up on your work surface. Align the zipper, *wrong side up*, along the top of the front unit. Align the pocket lining piece A2, *wrong side up*, over the zipper and the front unit. Pin. Using a zipper foot and

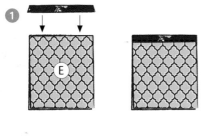

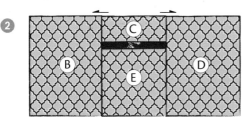

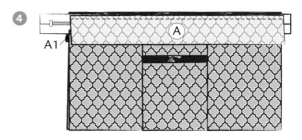

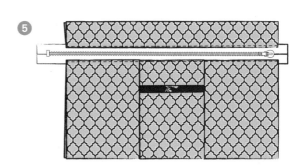

a ¼" seam allowance, sew along the top edge through all layers. Move the zipper pull as needed to make stitching along the zipper easier. **3**

5. Press the layers away from the zipper using low heat and the point of your iron.

6. Repeat with piece A and pocket lining piece A1 along the other edge of the zipper. (Make sure the right side of piece A is against the right side of the front unit.) **4**

7. Topstitch ⅛" from the seam on either side of the zipper, through all layers. **5**

8. With the right side facing up, layer the front unit made in the previous steps on the front pocket lining piece A3. Baste around the perimeter of the pieces through all layers. With right sides together, sew pieces H1 and H2 to either side of the unit and press the seam allowances outward. **6**

9. Position two 8" strips of 1"-wide nylon webbing along the bottom raw edge as shown and layer piece J on top, right sides together. Sew, backstitching over the straps for strength. **7**

10. Fold the 17" square (piece G) in half to make a piece 17" x 8½" and press. Prepare the 2" x 17" binding strip as in step 1, and stitch it over the fold of piece G.

11. Layer pocket G on piece F, right sides up. With right sides together, stitch pieces H3 and H4 to the sides of the unit. Press the seam allowances outward.

12. Stitch piece K to the bottom of the unit, right sides together. Press the seam allowances toward piece K. **8**

13. Layer the back unit and front unit right sides together as shown. Stitch around both sides and the bottom, leaving the top open. **9**

14. To box the bottom of the bag, flatten the corners

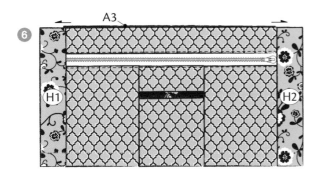

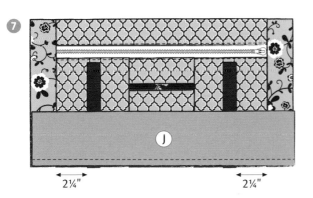

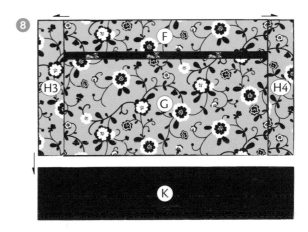

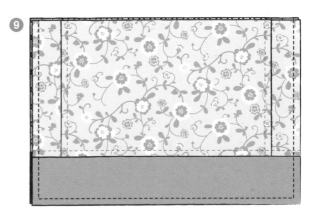

and align the seam allowances. Press. Measure 2" from each corner point and mark a line perpendicular to the seam. Sew across the line twice for strength. Trim the corners ¼" from the stitching and zigzag the edges to finish. ⑩

constructing the flap

1. Use the corner template on page 32 to mark the bottom corners on the outer flap and lining flap pieces. Trim the rounded corners.

2. With right sides together, stitch the outer flap and lining pieces together, leaving the straight edge open. Clip the seam allowances. ⑪

3. Turn the flap right side out, roll the seam (page 104), and press. Topstitch ⅛" from the sewn edge.

4. From the 1"-wide nylon webbing, cut two 10"-long

pieces. Fold each webbing piece in half, insert the female end of the side-release buckle, and then pin the webbing to the flap lining as shown. Using bobbin thread to match the outer fabric and top thread to match the webbing, stitch through all layers. ⑫

cutting for the lining

From the gray ripstop nylon, cut:
1 rectangle, 17" x 17" (lining pocket piece L)
2 rectangles, 17" x 11½" (lining pieces M and P)
4 strips, 3" x 11½" (lining side panels N1–N4)
2 strips, 21" x 4½" (pieces O and Q)

From the maroon cotton print, cut:
1 piece, 4¼" x 5" (key fob)
1 strip, 2" x 17" (inner pocket binding)

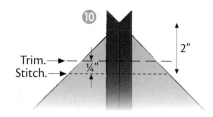

Trim. →
Stitch. →
¼"
2"

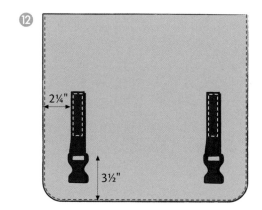

2¼"
3½"

constructing the lining

1. Fold piece L in half widthwise to make a piece 17" x 8½" and press. Prepare the 2" x 17" binding strip as in step 2 of "Constructing the Outer Bag," page 26, and stitch the binding over the fold.

2. Mark the stitching lines onto the front of piece L and layer it on piece M, right sides up. Pin. Topstitch through all layers along the marked lines to create pockets, backstitching at the beginning and end. ⑬

3. Sew pieces N1 and N2 to either side of the pocket unit, right sides together, and press the seam allowances outward. Sew piece O to the bottom of the unit and press the seam allowances toward piece O. ⑭

4. Sew pieces N3 and N4 to the sides of lining piece P, followed by piece Q. ⑮

5. With the two lining units right sides together, stitch around the sides and the bottom, leaving the top open and an 8" gap on one side. Backstitch twice on either side of the gap for strength. ⑯

6. Box the lining corners as you did in step 14 of "Constructing the Outer Bag."

7. To prepare the key fob, fold the 4¼" x 5" piece in half lengthwise, wrong sides together, and press. Open the piece and turn the raw edges in to meet the fold. Refold, enclosing the raw edges, and press. Topstitch along both long edges. Run this strap through the swivel hook and set aside.

cutting for the padded sleeve

From the ripstop nylon, cut:
1 piece, 46" x 18" (padding cover)

From the closed-cell foam, cut:
2 rectangles, 15½" x 10¾"

⑬
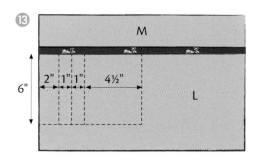

⑮
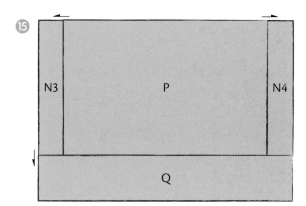

⑭
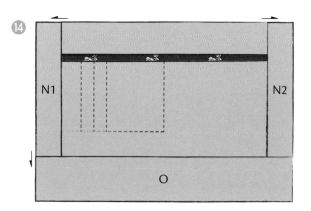

⑯
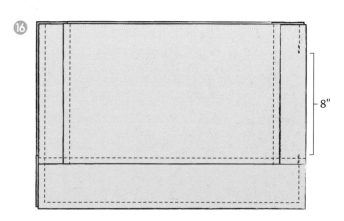

constructing the padded sleeve

If you don't need a padded inner sleeve, skip to the next section, "Putting the Bag Together."

1. Fold the 46" x 18" nylon piece in half widthwise. Stitch across the piece through both layers, 11" from the fold. Then stitch across 22" from the fold, creating two slots. **17**

2. Slide the foam pieces into the slots and center them.

3. Fold the unit in half so the foam pieces are together. Using a zipper foot, stitch the sides through all layers as close to the foam as possible. You should now have a lined foam "envelope" with a 1" seam allowance at the top, which will get sewn into the main bag. **18**

4. If using ripstop nylon or another no-fray (or low-fray) fabric, trim the side seam allowances to ⅛". If using cotton or another fabric that frays, trim to ¼" and stitch binding or bias tape along the

sides to enclose the raw edges. (Of course, you can bind the raw edges no matter what material you use.)

putting the bag together

I won't lie—this section is a doozy. You'll sew all of these layers together, and it's not easy, but I have several tips to ensure success. The most important thing is to layer the pieces in the correct order, because the lining, sleeve, flap, and outer bag are all sewn in one go. Another key is to go slowly and use *lots* of pins. There are several bulky areas where you may want to hand turn your machine. Don't be afraid to backstitch over seams and straps for extra strength. I recommend using a jeans needle to get through all the layers.

1. Turn the outer bag right side out, but leave the lining wrong side out. Place the outer bag inside

17

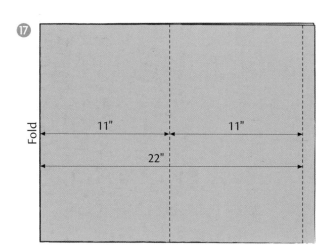

Fold

11"   11"

22"

18

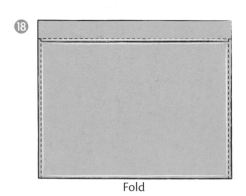

Fold

the lining, with the outer bag pocket and the lining pocket facing each other. Now sandwich the flap between the outer bag and the lining, with the outer flap fabric against the outer bag, and the flap lining against the bag lining. Slip your padded sleeve in, raw edges up, between the flap and the lining, with the opening of the sleeve against the flap. Align all top raw edges and pin liberally all the way around. **⑲**

2. From the 2"-wide nylon webbing, cut two strips 10" long and one strip 32" long. Weave one end of a 10" strip through a standard loop and fold it in half. Place the webbing in between the lining and the outer bag, centered on the side seam, with the raw ends sticking 3" beyond the raw edges of the other units. Pin. Repeat on the other side with the second 10" strip and a standard loop. Finally, slip the key fob between the lining and the outer bag at the end nearest the zipper pull. Align the raw edges and pin. **⑳**

3. Stitch the back seam first. Then stitch each side seam, backstitching over the straps. Finally, stitch the front seam. Stitching these seams separately helps keep everything in order and makes it easier to go back if you run into a problem.

4. Once the entire top seam has been stitched, turn the bag inside out through the gap in the lining and hand stitch the gap closed. Push the lining and padded sleeve down into the outer bag. It should look like a bag now!

5. Roll the entire top seam and press to get a nice finished edge. Topstitch ¼" from the seam, but do not stitch over the key fob.

6. To anchor the straps, stitch through all layers on either side of the bag as shown. **㉑**

7. Weave the male ends of the side-release buckles through the loose 1" webbing straps on the lower front of the bag. Fold the ends of the loose straps over ½" and zigzag twice to secure.

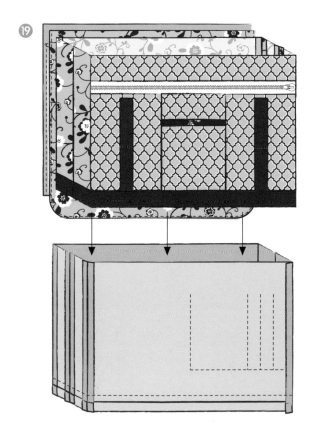

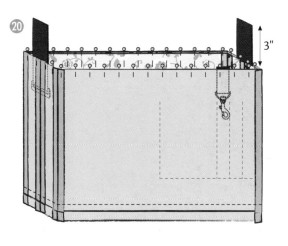

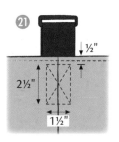

8. Fold over 3" at one end of the 32" length of webbing and thread it through one of the standard loops at the side of the bag so that the end of the webbing faces inward, not outward. Stitch as shown. ㉒

9. Run the other end of the webbing through the single-bar slide (a), then through the standard loop at the opposite side of the bag (b). Finally, weave the end through the single-bar slide again (c) and stitch the end (d) to the webbing underneath. ㉓

- -

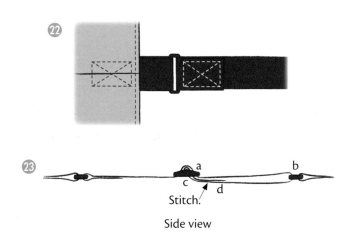

㉒

㉓
a
b
c
d
Stitch.

Side view

Bag Hardware

A great variety of hardware is readily available for bag making. Some of it may be unfamiliar, so a brief introduction is in order. Single-bar slides are used to make adjustable straps. Standard loops are single loops used for connecting straps or anchoring an adjustable strap. Side-release buckles, also called "parachute" buckles, make excellent bag closures. Swivel hooks are great as bag clips for wristlets and detachable straps. D-rings (not featured in these projects) are great for attaching a flat strap to another piece of hardware, such as a swivel hook.

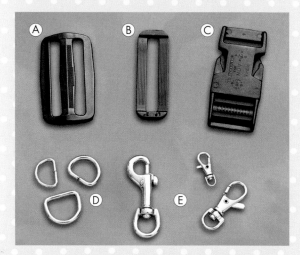

A. single-bar slide; B. standard loop;
C. side-release buckle; D. D-rings; E. swivel hooks

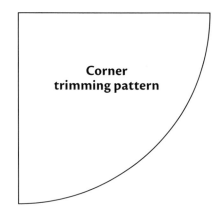

**Corner
trimming pattern**

cutting garden COASTERS

These bright floral coasters will add pop to your next spring soiree—and they're just as fun to put together as they are to show off! Wonky Log Cabin quilt blocks are made totally free-form, with no precise cutting or complex patterns to follow, so they are a good introduction to quiltmaking techniques. Bold prints and colors make these coasters great for spring and summer, but with seasonal fabrics, they're a perfect gift any time of year.

Designed and sewn by
Cassie Barden

Finished Size: 5" x 5"

materials

Scraps of at least 10 fabrics for Log Cabin blocks

Fat quarter or four 6" x 6" squares of cotton print for coaster backing

¼ yard of cotton print for coaster binding

12" x 12" scrap of batting

making the coasters

Use ¼" seam allowances.

1. Cut an uneven square with sides approximately 1½" to 2½" for one Log Cabin center. Cut an assortment of uneven strips in various lengths for the logs.

2. With right sides together, sew an uneven strip along the top of the center piece. Flip the strip open, press, and trim. Sew and trim a second strip to the side of the unit. ❶

3. Repeat, sewing strips clockwise around the center piece in the numerical order shown. Sew as many or as few strips onto the unit as you like, continuing in the same direction, until the shape is at least 5½" on all sides. ❷

4. Trim the finished unit to 5" x 5". ❸

5. Using an erasable fabric marker, mark straight quilting lines similar to those shown. There's no need to follow the illustration exactly; just mark lines that look good on your square. ❹

6. If you're using a fat quarter for the backing, cut four 6" squares. Refer to "Quiltmaking Basics" (page 108) to layer your Log Cabin square with a 6" batting square and a 6" backing square. Pin or baste the layers together. Quilt along the marked lines.

7. Trim the quilt "sandwich" to 5" x 5".

8. Refer to "Binding" (page 108) to prepare the binding strip, attach it to the coaster, and hand stitch it around the edge.

9. Repeat for the remaining coasters.

Trim.

Stitch.

paris afternoon
TEA SERVICE SET

Add a bit of Parisian elegance to afternoon (or morning or weekend) tea with this set of linens. A patchwork tea towel keeps the *très Francais macarons* fresh until you are ready to nibble, and embellished napkins are perfect for daintily wiping fingers. A tea-themed dish towel, stitched with the phrase "One always has time for tea and macarons" in French, gently dries your fancy dishes when the party wraps up. This set makes a wonderful gift for a tea-loving (or macaron-loving!) friend or, of course, for yourself.

Designed and sewn by
Cassie Barden

Finished Tea Towel: 14" x 14"
Finished Napkin: 11" x 11"
Finished Dish Towel: 16" x 23"

materials
Yardage is based on 42"-wide fabric.

1⅓ yards of unbleached linen for tea towel, napkins, and dish towel

¼ yard or fat quarter of cotton print for tea towel

4" length of ribbon for tea towel

Small button for tea towel

Embroidery floss to match cotton print for tea towel

Two packages of baby rickrack for napkins

Embroidery floss for dish towel: spring green, chocolate brown, lilac, sky blue, and pink

1 yard of 1¼" pom-pom trim for dish towel

9" x 15" piece of water-soluble stabilizer for dish towel

cutting
From the linen, cut:
2 squares, 7½" x 7½"
1 square, 14½" x 14½"
4 squares, 13" x 13"
1 rectangle, 18" x 25"

From the cotton print, cut:
2 squares, 7½" x 7½"

making the tea towel

Use ¼" seam allowances unless otherwise indicated.

1. With right sides together, sew each 7½" linen square to a cotton square and press the seam allowances open. Fold the length of ribbon in half to make a loop and pin to one of the units at the center seam. Layer the two units, right sides together and seams aligned, and pin. ❶

2. Sew the units together and press the seam allowances open.

3. Using three strands of embroidery floss and a backstitch (page 106), stitch a square in each linen patch ½" from the seams and ¾" from the raw edges. ❷

4. Layer the four-patch unit and the remaining linen square right sides together and pin. Stitch around the perimeter, leaving a 4" gap along one edge. Clip the corners, turn, and press. Close the gap using a ladder stitch (page 107).

5. Using the embroidery floss, insert the needle between the layers near the center, burying a small knot where the ribbon is sewn into the seam. Push the needle through the back and the button at the center, then bring the needle to the front, through the center of the ribbon. Make two or three stitches in this manner. Secure the thread by taking several tiny stitches on the back, under the button. ❸

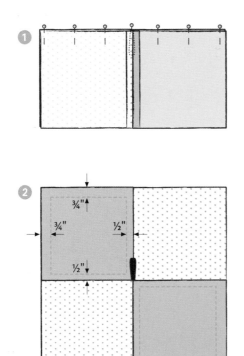

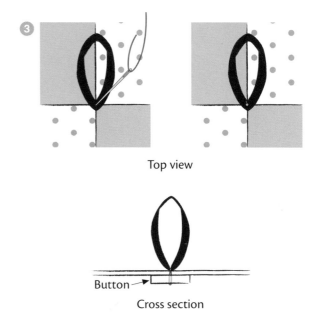

Top view

Button →

Cross section

3. Unfold the corners. Using the creases as guides, trim the corners as shown. ⑤

4. Refold each edge along the first fold line. ⑥

5. Fold each corner down at the point where the second fold lines intersect and pin. ⑦

6. Fold the edges again, this time along the second fold lines, to create a mitered corner. Pin. ⑧

7. Using thread to match the linen, machine stitch the folded edges. ⑨

8. Turn the napkin to the right side. Using top thread to match the rickrack and bobbin thread to match the linen, stitch the rickrack over the previous stitching, pivoting at the corners. When you get to the beginning, trim the rickrack so it just overlaps the start, stitch to the end, and backstitch.

making the linen napkins

1. Turn under ½" along each edge of a 13" napkin square and press. ④

2. Turn under ½" again and press.

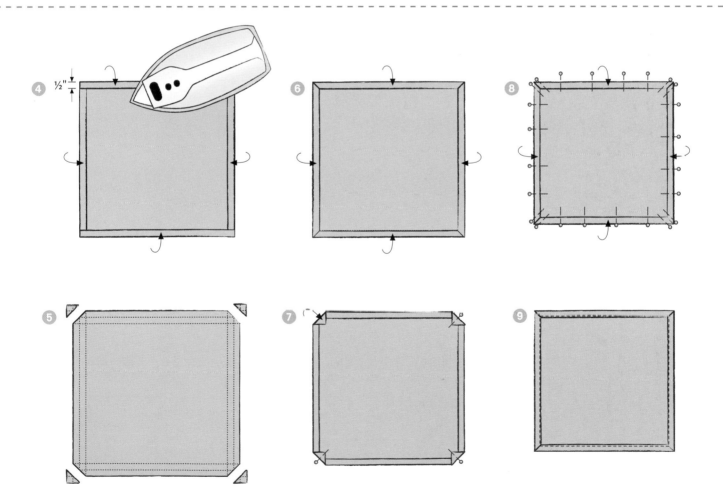

Il y a toujours assez de temps pour du thé et des macarons!

making the embroidered dish towel

1. Hem the perimeter of the 18" x 25" linen rectangle as in steps 1–7 for the linen napkins (page 39).

2. Trace the embroidery design at right onto the water-soluble stabilizer. Pin the stabilizer with the design approximately 2" from the bottom and 6¼" from either side. Using the colors shown in the stitching diagram and three strands of floss, embroider the design. I used a backstitch for the entire design, except for the steam swirls, where I used a very tiny running stitch.

3. Using top thread to match the trim and bobbin thread to match the linen, stitch the "ribbon" portion of the pom-pom trim to the short edges of the towel, sewing from the hemmed side.

Embroidery pattern

secret ingredient APRON

You'll look sweet as pie in this generously sized, full-length apron. Whether you're baking a soufflé or serving strawberry shortcake, the bib and gathered skirts will protect your clothes from your culinary concoctions. Little details like the buttons and pleats on the pocket are the icing on the cake of this fun pattern.

Designed by Adrienne Smitke;
sewn by Judy Smitke

Finished Size: Adult women's; one size fits most.

materials

Yardage is based on 42"-wide fabric.

1⅛ yards of strawberry print for bib, top skirt, and pocket

1 yard of red polka-dot fabric for waistband, waist ties, neck strap, and pocket trim

⅝ yard of pale green print for underskirt

½ yard of cotton batiste for bib interlining

¼ yard of 20"-wide lightweight fusible interfacing

Two buttons, ½" diameter, for bib and pocket

cutting

From the strawberry print, cut:
1 rectangle, 17" x 30"
2 rectangles, 6" x 8"
2 rectangles, 12½" x 16"

From the pale green print, cut:
1 rectangle, 18½" x 36"

From the red polka-dot fabric, cut:
1 rectangle, 3" x 7"
4 strips, 3½" x 36"
2 strips, 4" x 21"
1 strip, 6" x 26"

From the cotton batiste:
1 rectangle, 16" x 12½"

From the interfacing:
1 strip, 3½" x 20"

making the apron skirts

Use ½" seam allowances unless otherwise indicated.

1. Hem both short sides of the 17" x 30" strawberry print top skirt by turning under the raw edge ¼" and pressing, then turning under ¼" again and topstitching. Hem the bottom edge in the same manner. Repeat with the 18½" x 36" pale green print underskirt.

2. With the top skirt right side up, sew a long basting stitch ¼" from the upper edge. Sew a second row of stitching ⅜" from the edge. Do not trim the thread tails at either end. ❶

3. Pick up only the *front* tails at either end of the second row of stitching and pull gently with one hand to gather the fabric. Use the thumb and forefinger of your other hand to distribute the gathers evenly. Continue to gather the skirt until it measures 17" wide. ❷

4. Repeat steps 2 and 3 with the underskirt, gathering until it is 20" wide.

5. For the pocket trim, turn under ½" on both long edges of a 3" x 7" red polka-dot rectangle and press. Fold the pocket trim in half lengthwise, right sides together and matching the folded edges. Sew each short side, leaving the long edges open. Trim the seam allowances to ¼", trim the corners, and turn right side out. Press.

6. With the 6" x 8" strawberry print rectangles right sides together, use the pocket corner template on page 45 to mark and trim the bottom corners. Sew the rectangles, leaving the top edge open. Clip the curves, being careful not to cut the stitching, and turn right side out. Press. ❸

7. Using an erasable marking tool, mark the center of the pocket and ½" on either side of the center. To make the pleat, hold both layers together and bring each outer line to meet the center line. Pin at the top and farther down the pleats to keep the upper edge straight. Baste across the top of the pocket using a ¼" seam allowance. ❹

8. Slip approximately ½" of the raw pocket edges inside the open edges of the pocket trim. Pin. Topstitch ⅛" around the pocket trim, catching the folded edges in the seam. ❺

9. Pin the pocket to the top skirt approximately 3" from the upper edge and off to one side. Using matching thread, topstitch a scant ⅛" around the pocket, stitching over the first stitching on the trim.

10. Center the top skirt on the underskirt, aligning the gathered edges. Pin.

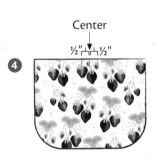

Center
½" ½"

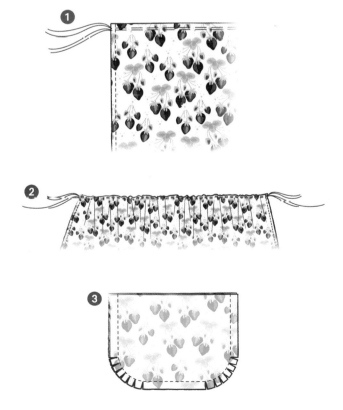

making the ties and waistband

1. For the waist ties, pin each 3½" x 36" red polka-dot strip right sides together. Using the 45° line on your ruler, trim one short end. Make one and one reversed. ❻

2. Sew three sides of each strip, leaving the straight end open. Trim the corners and turn each tie right side out. Press. Topstitch ⅛" from the edges.

3. For the waistband, follow the manufacturer's instructions to fuse a 3½" x 20" strip of lightweight interfacing to the wrong side of a 4" x 21" red polka-dot strip, centering the interfacing lengthwise and aligning it with the upper edge of the strip.

4. Use the interfacing as a guide to fold the bottom edge of the strip ½" to the wrong side. Press. Fold the remaining red polka-dot strip ½" to the wrong side and press. ❼

5. Pin the strips right sides together, sandwiching a waist tie between the layers at either short end, ¼" from the folded edge. *Sew the sides of the waistband only*, leaving the top and bottom open. ❽

6. Slip the two gathered skirts in between the waistbands, centering the skirts and aligning all raw edges. Pin. *Sew this top seam only*, leaving the folded edges free. ❾

7. Trim the corners and turn the waistband right side out. Press.

Half-Apron Alternative
Only need a half-length apron? Guess what? You're done! Topstitch the waistband along the folded edges, and you're ready to get back into the kitchen.

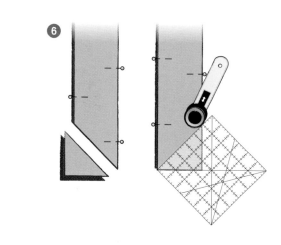

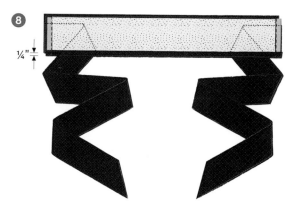

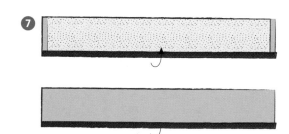

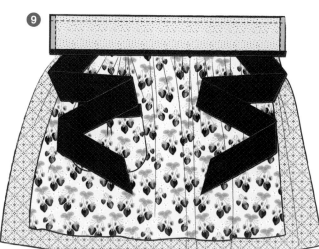

making the apron bib

1. To make the neck strap, fold the 6" x 26" red polka-dot strip in half lengthwise, wrong sides together, and press. Open the strip and turn the raw edges in to meet the fold. Refold, enclosing the raw edges, and press. Topstitch the strip ⅛" from the folded edges. **10**

2. Baste the 16" x 12½" piece of cotton batiste to the wrong side of one strawberry print rectangle for the bib front. With the strawberry rectangles right sides together, mark the top edge 2" from either corner. Draw a line from these marks to the bottom corners of the rectangles. Trim on the lines. **11**

3. Pin the strap ends a *generous* ½" from either side at the top of the bib. Try on the bib and adjust the length of the strap if necessary. I have a curvier figure, so I trimmed my strap to 20", but you may want to make your strap shorter.

4. With right sides togther and the neck strap sandwiched between the bib pieces, sew the sides and the top of the bib, leaving the bottom open. Trim the corners, turn right side out, and press. **12**

5. With the bib right side up, mark the center of the top and 1" on either side of the center. Pleat the bib as you did the pocket and pin. Topstitch ⅛" from the sides and upper edge.

finishing the apron

1. Slip a generous ½" of the bottom edge of the bib between the open edges of the waistband, making sure the bib is centered. Pin. Topstitch ⅛" from all edges of the waistband, catching the bib in the stitching and backstitching at the beginning and end.

2. Hand stitch a ½" button at the center of the bib pleat and the pocket pleat.

10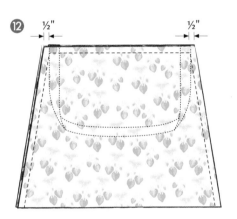

12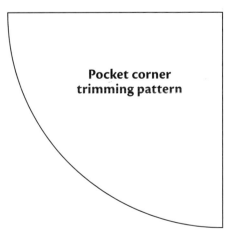

11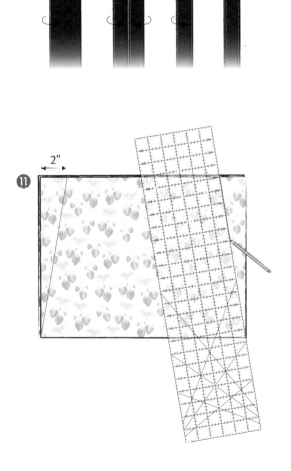

Pocket corner trimming pattern

wild strawberry POT HOLDER

Pot holders are a dime a dozen at the kitchen store, but with a little custom appliqué, a handmade pot holder makes a wonderful—and personal—housewarming gift. The coordinating trim really kicks things up a notch, but if you use something besides rickrack, just make sure it's heat-safe.

Designed and sewn by
Cassie Barden

Finished Size: 9" x 9"

materials

Yardage is based on 42"-wide fabric.

½ yard of brown wood-grain print for pocket front and binding

⅓ yard or fat quarter of red gingham for pocket lining and pot holder back

10" x 10" scrap or fat quarter of floral print for pot holder front

⅓ yard of insulated batting

11" length of ¾"-wide red rickrack

8" x 8" square of paper-backed fusible web

cutting

From the brown wood-grain print, cut:
1 square, 9" x 9"
1 strip, 2½" x 11"
1 strip, 2½" x 42"

From the red gingham, cut:
2 squares, 9" x 9"

From the floral print, cut:
1 square, 9" x 9"

From the insulated batting, cut:
4 squares, 9" x 9"

preparing the layers

Use ¼" seam allowances.

1. Referring to "The Quilt Sandwich" (page 108), stack your 9" squares into two groups as shown. Note the orientation of the fabric squares to ensure you trim the correct corners in the next step. **1**

2. Set the batting squares aside, being careful to keep the fabric squares oriented correctly. Using the corner template on page 49 and an erasable fabric marker, mark the three corners indicated on each fabric square. The insulated batting is difficult to mark, so once you've marked the cotton fabrics, pin one piece of fabric to one batting square and trim both layers at once. **2**

3. Stack your "quilt sandwiches" again as shown in illustration 1, below, and set the pot holder pieces aside to work on the front pocket.

making the pocket

1. With the pocket front and pocket lining wrong sides together, measure and mark a point 6" from the square corner, along the top and left edges. Draw a line from mark to mark and trim on the line. Trim two batting squares in the same way. **3**

2. Referring to "Appliqué" (page 105) and the patterns (page 49), fuse the strawberry appliqué to the wood-grain pocket piece, starting with the strawberry, and then the hull. Machine appliqué the pieces.

3. Restack the pocket and batting pieces and, using a walking foot, baste a scant ¼" around the perimeter.

4. Pin the rickrack to the diagonal edge of the pocket, aligning the top edge of the rickrack with the raw edges.

5. Refer to "Binding" (page 108) to prepare your 11" binding strip and machine stitch it to the diagonal

---

Pocket lining (wrong side up) · 2 layers insulated batting

Pocket front (right side up)

Pocket

Pot holder back (wrong side up) · 2 layers insulated batting

Pot holder front (right side up)

Pot holder

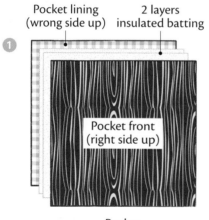

Trim.

6" · 6"

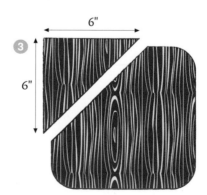

edge of the red gingham lining. Fold the binding to the front of the pocket and stitch through all layers. Trim the ends even with the pocket. **4**

assembling the pot holder

1. Using a walking foot, baste a scant ¼" around the perimeter of the pot holder stack. Layer the pocket on the pot holder, carefully aligning the curved edges, and secure with long pins or metal hair clips.

2. Prepare the 42" wood-grain binding strip and turn the pot holder over so the red gingham faces up. Using a walking foot, begin sewing the binding at the square corner of the pot holder. Stitch around the perimeter, stopping several inches before you reach the corner again. **5**

3. Fold a few inches of the beginning binding away from the pot holder and finger-press. Continue stitching, stopping just at the "bump" of the binding fold and backstitching. **6**

4. Turn the pot holder over and fold the binding to the front. Pin the binding, making small tucks at the rounded corners. Starting at the corner where the binding overlaps itself, stitch close to the folded edge. When you reach the beginning corner again, fold the raw edges of the binding in and continue stitching to the end. **7**

5. Trim the binding tail so the loop is the desired length, about 3". Using a short zigzag stitch, sew the raw end of the tail closed. Turn the tail down and tack it to the back of the pot holder. **8**

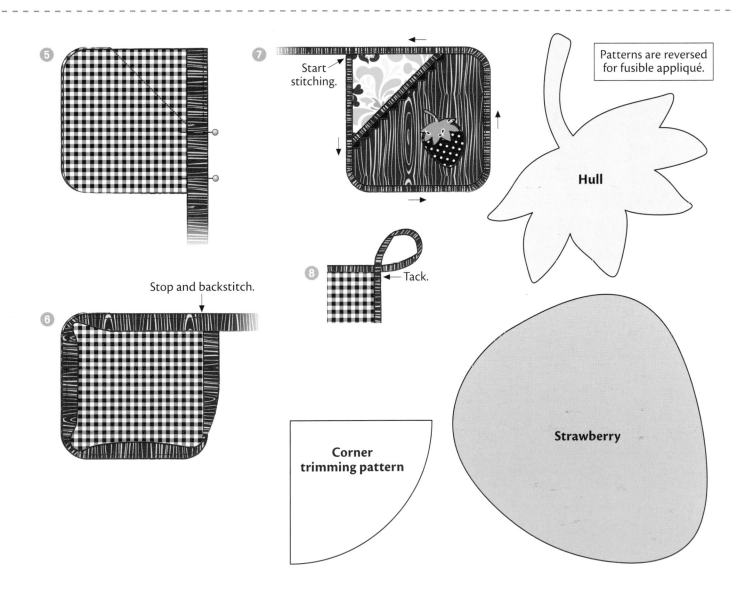

Patterns are reversed for fusible appliqué.

Hull

Start stitching.

Tack.

Stop and backstitch.

Corner trimming pattern

Strawberry

mustachioed man IPAD CASE

Made with 3 mm thick 100% wool felt, this envelope-style case is a modern, luxurious, and quirky way to protect your tablet in style. Try other appliqué designs to suit different personalities and consider experimenting with cotton prints, patterned wool, or vinyl for the appliqués. The 3 mm felt is available online in a variety of colors, by the yard as well as in single sheets. See "Online Resources" (page 110). My case was made to fit my iPad, but this simple project is easy to resize to fit your tablet.

Designed and sewn by
Cassie Barden

Finished Size: 8¼" x 10½"

materials

14" x 18" piece or two sheets, at least 9" x 14", of 3 mm dark gray felt for case front and back

2" x 6" piece of 1 mm brown felt for mustache

2" x 6" piece of 1 mm green felt for necktie

6" length of black ½"-wide Velcro

cutting

Referring to "Making Templates and Transferring Designs" (page 104), use the templates on page 52 to cut out the appliqué pieces.

From the dark gray felt, cut:
1 rectangle, 8¼" x 10½"
1 rectangle, 8¼" x 13"

From the brown felt, cut:
1 mustache

From the green felt, cut:
1 necktie

making the case

1. Measure, mark, and trim one short end of the 8¼" x 13" gray felt rectangle to make the flap. ❶

2. Pin and stitch the soft (loop) side of the Velcro ¼" from the top of the flap. Stitch the stiff (hook) side to the other rectangle, 1¾" from the top. ❷

3. Center and pin the mustache and tie pieces as shown to the felt piece with the flap, on the side *without* the Velcro, using small, thin pins. Don't pin all the way through the thick felt; just dip in a bit and then come back up. You can also swipe an acid-free glue stick across the back of the appliqué for a temporary hold. ❸

4. Using a satin stitch and matching thread, machine appliqué the pieces to the felt.

5. Layer the pieces wrong sides together. Using a ¼" seam allowance, stitch around the sides and bottom, backstitching at the beginning and end. ❹

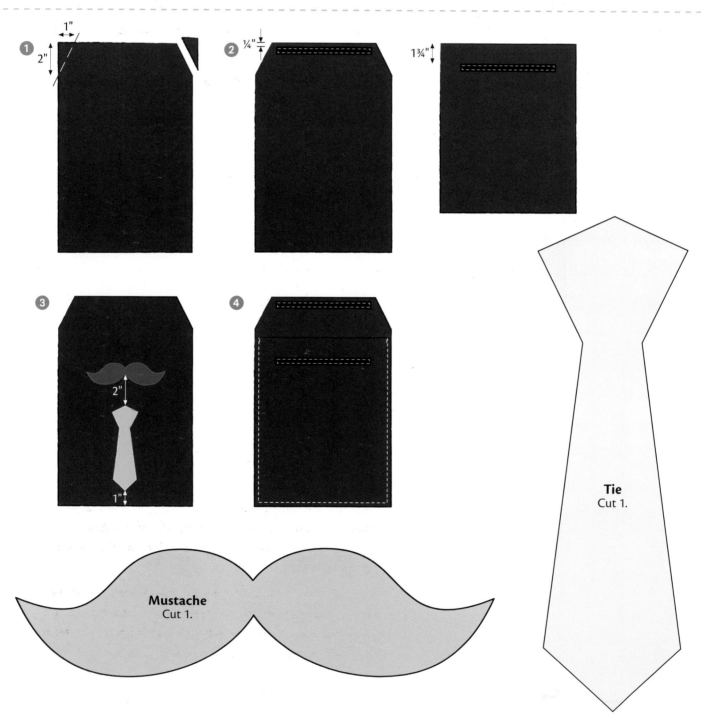

Mustache Cut 1.

Tie Cut 1.

flotsam and jetsam BOX BAG

Whether filled with cosmetics, a small knitting project, or your daily accessories, this box-style bag is the perfect pouch for carrying all your odds and ends when you're on the go. While the techniques used to make this bag aren't difficult, the more precise your sewing, the better your finished bag, so take your time to measure carefully and sew accurately.

Designed and sewn by
Adrienne Smitke

Finished Size: 4" x 6" x 4¾"

materials
Yardage is based on 42"-wide fabric.

One fat quarter of medium-weight novelty print for bag exterior

One fat quarter of orange polka-dot fabric for bag lining

⅛ yard *or* fat quarter of teal striped fabric for contrast pieces and strap

½ yard of 20"-wide medium-weight fusible interfacing

12" zipper

cutting
From the novelty print, cut:
1 rectangle, 12" x 16½"
1 strip, 2" x 12"

From the orange polka-dot fabric, cut:
1 rectangle, 12" x 18½"
2 strips, 2½" x 21"

From the teal striped fabric, cut:
3 strips, 1½" x 12"

From the interfacing, cut:
1 rectangle, 12" x 16½"
2 strips, 1½" x 12"

making the body of the bag
Use ¼" seam allowances.

1. Follow the manufacturer's instructions to fuse the large interfacing rectangle to the wrong side of the large novelty print rectangle. Fuse the interfacing strips to two of the teal strips.

2. To make the bag exterior, sew the fused teal strips on the short sides of the novelty print rectangle. Press the seam allowances toward the novelty print and topstitch ⅛" from the seam using a contrasting thread.

3. Align the zipper, right side up, along the top edge of the orange polka-dot rectangle, also right side up. Align the bag exterior (with the teal strip at the top), *wrong side up*, over the zipper and the lining. Pin. **1**

4. Using a zipper foot and a ¼" seam allowance, sew through all layers. Move the zipper pull as needed to make stitching along the zipper easier.

5. Press the fabrics away from the zipper using low heat and the point of your iron. Topstitch the teal strip a scant ⅛" from the zipper. **2**

(Un)Matching Threads

When you know both sides of a seam are going to show (such as when you're topstitching next to a zipper), match your top thread to the top fabric and your bobbin thread to the bottom fabric. It's little details like this that will make your bag stand out!

6. To sew the other side of the zipper, arrange the layers in the same order as in step 3. Start by folding the bag exterior in half, right sides together, aligning the raw edge of the teal strip with the remaining edge of the zipper. Next, fold the orange polka-dot lining in half, right sides together, also aligning its raw edge with the remaining edge of the zipper. Pin. You'll have two loops of fabric with the zipper sandwiched in between. **3**

7. Using your zipper foot, sew along the top edge through all layers. Remember to move the zipper pull to make stitching along the zipper easier.

8. With the zipper open, turn the tube right side out, pushing the orange polka-dot lining inside the tube. Topstitch the other teal strip as you did in step 5.

making the zipper tab and handle

1. Using your standard presser foot, sew the 2" x 12" novelty print strip and the remaining 1½" x 12" teal strip right sides together along one long edge. Sew the remaining edges right sides together to make a tube.

2. Turn the tube right side out. Press flat, centering the teal strip. Topstitch ¼" from each long edge. **4**

3. Trim a 3½" piece of this strip for the zipper tab. Fold the piece in half, teal stripe on the outside, and baste the raw edges together.

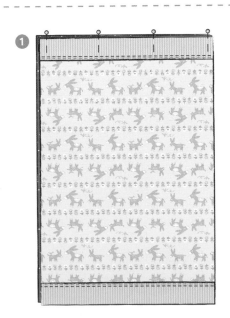

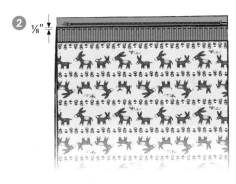
⅛"

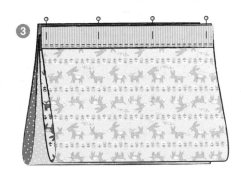

¼"

boxing the corners

1. Close the zipper and turn the tube, lining side out. With the zipper teeth at the very top, press a crease at the bottom of the bag. **5**

2. Open the tube and center the zipper, using the crease you just pressed as a guide.

3. Tuck the zipper tab inside the tube, centering it under the zipper pull and using the crease as a guide. Align the raw edges and pin. **6**

4. Stitch across the end of the tube, moving the zipper pull a few inches so it doesn't interfere with the seam, and backstitching over the zipper tape and tab; see "Stitching Across a Zipper" (facing page). (If you're worried about backstitching through all those layers, you can always go back and sew a second seam.) Trim any excess zipper.

5. Unzip the zipper halfway. (You will turn the bag right side out through the open zipper, so don't forget this important step!) Stitch across the opposite edges of the tube in the same manner.

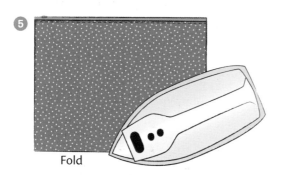

5

Fold

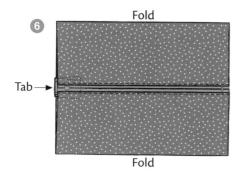

6

Fold

Tab →

Fold

6. To finish the raw edges on the lining, fold a 2½" x 21" lining strip in half lengthwise, wrong sides together, and press. Open the strip and fold the raw edges in to meet the fold. Refold, enclosing the raw edges, and press. Center and sandwich a 7" length of the strip over the raw seam allowances of one of the side seams. (The strip won't cover the full length of the seam; you'll finish the other edges after boxing the corners.) Topstitch close to the folded edges, through all layers. Repeat with the remaining strip on the opposite seam.

Stitching Across a Zipper

Be cautious when stitching across a zipper. I like to hand turn my machine to avoid hitting one of the zipper teeth with the needle. Backstitch carefully to secure the teeth.

7. Mark 2" on either side of the zipper teeth on each edge. (This measurement determines the shape of your bag. For a wider, shallower bag, make the marks farther apart.) Press the fold on either long edge of the bag to make a crease. **7**

8. On the edge with the zipper tab, reach into one corner and flatten it so the seam matches the just-pressed crease, forming a triangle. Pin the triangle flat, making sure the finished edges are pressed *away* from the zipper. Using the mark you made in step 7 as a guide, draw a line across the triangle, perpendicular to the seam.

9. Sew along the marked line, backstitching at either end and across the seam allowances. Trim the corners ¼" from the stitching and finish the raw edges with a length of the folded strip. Repeat for the nearby corner. **8**

10. At the other end of the tube, repeat step 8, but *don't* sew across the corners. Insert approximately 1" of the bag handle into one of the corner triangles you've created, making sure the teal strip on the handle faces toward the center of the bag. Insert the other end of the handle in the opposite corner triangle. Pin from the outside of the bag. This step takes some fiddling to get just right. Turn the bag right side out, if needed, to adjust the placement.

11. Stitch each corner, trim, and finish the edges. Now turn your bag right side out and wait for the compliments to start rolling in!

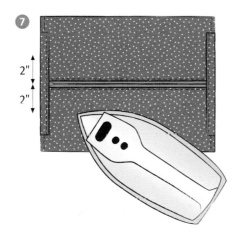

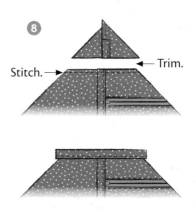

Stitch. → ← Trim.

literary genius
E-READER COVER

I'm a gadget geek *and* a craft geek, so the first thing I think when I get a new toy is, "This needs a handmade case!" This clever, simple cover is a great way to protect your e-reader. It feels nice in your hands when you're reading, it's a wonderful showcase for a favorite fabric, and it's quick enough to make that you can outfit all the members of your book club with custom covers of their own.

Designed and sewn by
Cassie Barden

Finished Size: 5½" x 8½" when folded

Note: *I've included measurements for the popular third generation Amazon Kindle (7.5" tall) and the first and second generations Barnes & Noble Nook (7.7" tall). The Nook measurements are shown in brackets. Construction is the same for both readers.*

materials

Yardage is based on 42"-wide fabric.

½ yard of turquoise cotton canvas print for case exterior

⅜ yard of purple polka-dot fabric for case interior

½ yard of 20"-wide medium-weight fusible interfacing*

Two pieces, 3" long, of ⅜"-wide elastic**

4" length of sew-in ⅝"-wide Velcro

If you use quilting cottons instead of cotton canvas, I recommend a slightly heavier-weight interfacing.

**Match the elastic to the e-reader, not to the fabric.*

cutting

From the turquoise cotton canvas print, cut:

1 rectangle, 15" x 8¾" [15" x 9"]

1 rectangle, 3" x 5"

2 squares, 2½" x 2½"

From the purple polka-dot fabric, cut:

1 rectangle, 9½" x 8¾" [9½" x 9"]

1 rectangle, 6" x 8¾" [6" x 9"]

1 rectangle, 3" x 5"

From the interfacing, cut:

1 rectangle, 9½" x 8¾" [9½" x 9"]

1 rectangle, 6" x 8¾" [6" x 9"]

1 rectangle, 3" x 5"

2 squares, 2½" x 2½"

making the case

Use ¼" seam allowances unless otherwise indicated.

1. Following the manufacturer's instructions, fuse all but the 2½" x 2½" squares of fusible interfacing to the wrong side of the corresponding lining pieces. Fuse the small interfacing squares to the wrong side of the corresponding turquoise print squares.

2. Press each small square in half, wrong sides together, to make a triangle.

3. Pin one piece of elastic to the upper-left corner of the 6" x 8¾" [6" x 9"] polka-dot lining rectangle, and one folded triangle to the lower-left corner. ❶

4. With right sides together, stitch the 9½" x 8¾" [9½" x 9"] lining piece to the 6" x 8¾" [6" x 9"] lining piece along the 9" edges. Press the seam allowances open. ❷

5. Sew the soft (loop) Velcro piece to the 3" x 5" polka-dot lining rectangle ½" from the right edge and centered vertically. ❸

6. With right sides together, stitch the 3" x 5" turquoise print and polka-dot lining rectangles together around three sides, leaving the edge without the Velcro open. Trim the corners, turn right side out, and press.

7. Pin the second piece of elastic to the upper-right corner of the lining. Pin the second triangle to the lower-right corner. Pin the flap to the right edge, lining to lining, with the flap centered vertically. ❹

8. With right sides together and raw edges aligned, pin the large turquoise print rectangle to the entire lining unit. Stitch around the perimeter, leaving a 4" gap along the lower-left edge (the area away from the triangles) and backstitching at the beginning and end.

9. Clip the corners, turn right side out, and roll the seams (page 104). Fold in and press the seam allowances on the gap and pin close to the edge.

1½"

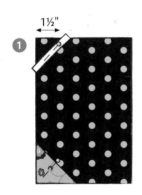

½"

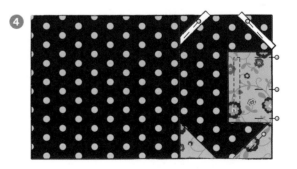

10. Place your e-reader in the case. Don't worry if it's a bit loose; just center it within the triangle pockets and elastic. Now fold over the left edge to create the vertical pocket, and then fold again over the reader. Adjust the pocket until everything lines up along the right edge and the case looks square. Pin the pocket to hold it temporarily, and then place a pin at the top and bottom of the vertical fold to mark it.

11. Pin the rough (hook) piece of Velcro to the front cover so it corresponds to the Velcro on the flap. Unfold the cover and remove the e-reader. Stitch the Velcro strip.

12. Refold the pocket, using the pins from step 10 as a guide, and pin. Topstitch a scant ⅛" around the cover perimeter, including the flap. **5**

ladybug COIN PURSE

Never dig for coins under the couch cushions or at the bottom of your bag again. This cute coin purse will store them safely, and you'll be looking for reasons to pay for things in pennies just so you can show it off.

Designed and sewn by
Adrienne Smitke

Finished Size: 4½" diameter

materials

¼ yard or fat quarter of red print for ladybug body

10" square of black felt for purse back, ladybug head, and spots

7" black zipper

Matching thread or one skein of black embroidery floss

Two buttons, 11 mm (⁷⁄₁₆") diameter, for eyes

Pinking shears (optional)

cutting

Referring to "Making Templates and Transferring Designs" (page 104), use the templates on page 65 to cut out the pieces.

From the black felt, cut:
1 body circle
1 head
2 spots

From the red print fabric, cut:
2 body circles

making the ladybug

Use ½" seam allowances unless otherwise indicated.

1. To make the wings, fold a red body circle in half, wrong sides together, and press. Pin the folded edge of one circle to the right side of the zipper, lining up the edge of the circle with the zipper stop. Using a zipper foot and a ¼" seam allowance, stitch through all layers, backstitching at the beginning and end. Finger-press the seam away from the zipper and topstitch a scant ⅛" from the seam. Repeat with the remaining red circle on the other side of the zipper. ①

2. Pin the black felt head piece to the body, aligning the curves. Topstitch by machine or hand stitch using a blanket stitch (page 106) and black embroidery floss. See "Stitching Across a Zipper" (page 57), disregarding the instruction to backstitch. Attach the spots using the same method, keeping them at least ⅞" from the curved edges. ②

3. Unzip the zipper a few inches so you can turn the case right side out once it's stitched. Pin the red body to the black felt circle, right sides together and raw edges aligned. At the open end of the zipper, pin the zipper tape so the teeth are just touching.

4. Sew around the perimeter. Trim the seam allowances, pinking the cotton fabrics, if desired, to keep them from fraying. Carefully trim the excess zipper beyond the seam allowances. Clip the curves approximately every ½", being careful not to cut the stitching. ③

5. Turn the case right side out and roll the seam (page 104) to smooth the curved edges. Attach the buttons for the eyes.

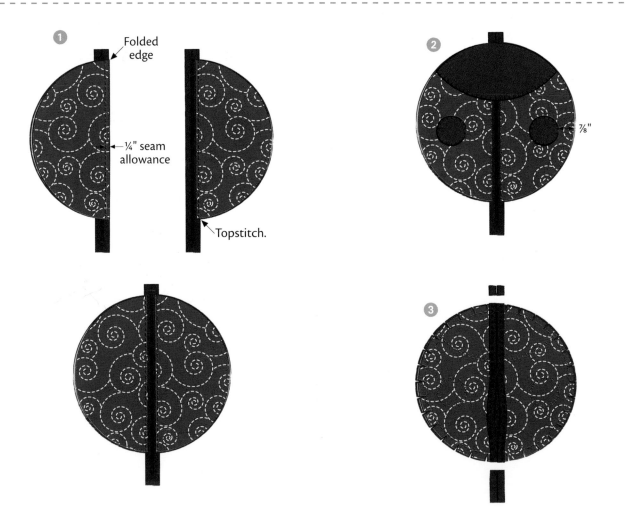

Ladybug head
Cut 1 from black felt.

Spot
Cut 2 from
black felt.

Ladybug body
Cut 1 from black felt
and 2 from red print.

½" seam allowance

wanderlust POCKETBOOK

This cute pocketbook-style wallet holds everything you'll need at your fingertips to travel the world. With plenty of pockets for your passport, tickets, and ID cards, you'll never have to go digging for important travel documents again. Plus, there are no metal parts to hold you up in security lines, and the wrist strap ensures your valuables won't wander away.

Designed and sewn by
Adrienne Smitke

Finished Size: 5½" x 8½" when folded

materials

Yardage is based on 42"-wide fabric.

½ yard of airplane-and-plaid print for pocketbook exterior

One fat quarter of red polka-dot fabric for lining and interior pocket

One fat quarter of striped linen for lining

One fat quarter of aqua polka-dot fabric for interior pockets

Scrap of red floral, at least 5" x 10", for card pocket

Scrap of red geometric print, at least 6" x 11", for flap lining

¾ yard of 20"-wide lightweight fusible interfacing

¾ yard of 20"-wide heavyweight fusible interfacing

One button, ¾" diameter

6" length of elastic cord

6" length of ⅝"-wide Velcro

cutting

From the airplane-and-plaid print, cut:
1 rectangle, 15" x 9½" (pocketbook exterior)
1 strip, 3" x 15" (wrist strap)

From the red polka-dot fabric, cut:
1 rectangle, 6¼" x 9½" (ticket pocket)
1 rectangle, 10" x 9½" (money pocket)

From the striped linen, cut:
1 rectangle, 12" x 9½" (lining)
1 rectangle, 6¼" x 9½" (ticket-pocket lining)

From the aqua polka-dot fabric, cut:
1 rectangle, 4½" x 9½" (card pocket)
1 rectangle, 5½" x 8" (passport pocket)

From the red floral, cut:
1 rectangle, 4½" x 9½" (card pocket)

From the red geometric print, cut:
1 rectangle, 5" x 9½" (flap lining)

From the lightweight interfacing, cut:

1 rectangle, 12" x 9½" (lining)

1 rectangle, 6¼" x 9½" (ticket pocket)

2 rectangles, 2¼" x 9½" (card pockets)

1 rectangle, 5½" x 4" (passport pocket)

1 rectangle, 5" x 9½" (money pocket)

From the heavyweight interfacing, cut:

1 rectangle, 15" x 9½" (exterior)

1 rectangle, 5" x 9½" (flap lining)

The Patchwork Effect

The fabric I chose for the pocketbook exterior featured stripes of multiple designs. If you want to reproduce this patchwork look with your own fabric, try piecing strips of varying widths, each 15" long, until you have a 9½" rectangle. You can use many fabrics or just a few to create your own effect.

making the pockets

Use ½" seam allowances.

1. To make the ticket pocket, follow the manufacturer's instructions to fuse a 6¼" x 9½" interfacing rectangle to the wrong side of the 6¼" x 9½" red polka-dot rectangle.

2. On the wrong side of the 6¼" x 9½" striped linen rectangle, mark 1" from the upper-left corner and 4½" from the lower-right corner. Connect the marks. With right sides together, pin the linen rectangle and the polka-dot rectangle. Sew across the top until you reach the marked line, pivot, sew on the marked line until ½" from the right edge, pivot, and finish sewing to the bottom of the pocket. Trim ½" from the marked line, clip the corners, and turn right side out. **1**

3. Topstitch ⅛" around the sewn edges of the pocket.

4. To make the passport pocket, fold the 5½" x 8" aqua polka-dot rectangle right sides together so it measures 5½" x 4". Fuse the 5½" x 4" interfacing rectangle to one side of the folded rectangle. Fold the elastic cord in half to create a loop and slip it between the two layers, centering the raw ends on the long open side. Pin to secure the elastic. Stitch around the three open sides, backstitching over the cord and leaving a 2" gap on one short side. **2**

5. Clip the corners and turn the pocket right side out through the gap. Roll the seams (page 104) and press. Topstitch ⅛" around the pocket, closing the gap.

6. Topstitch the passport pocket onto the ticket pocket, centering it ¾" from the bottom raw edge. Place your passport in the pocket to make sure the fit is snug. Sew the button just above the passport so the elastic loop will hook the button without pulling the pocket out of shape.

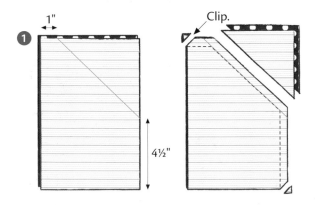

1"

1

4½"

Clip.

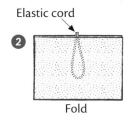

Elastic cord

2

Fold

2"

7. To make the money pocket, fold the 10" x 9½" red polka-dot rectangle *wrong sides together* so it measures 5" x 9½". Topstitch ⅛" from the fold.

8. To make the first card pocket, fold the 4½" x 9½" red floral rectangle *right sides together* so it measures 2¼" x 9½". Sew the long raw edges together. Turn the pocket right side out, roll the seam, and press flat. Topstitch ⅛" from the fold. Pin the floral card pocket to the red polka-dot money pocket 2" below the folded edge. Topstitch the card pocket to the money pocket, stitching a scant ⅛" from the bottom. ❸

9. For the second card pocket, fold the 4½" x 9½" aqua polka-dot rectangle *wrong sides* together so it measures 2¼" x 9½". Topstitch the pocket ⅛" from the fold. You don't need to sew the bottom edge of this pocket because it will be caught in the seam later.

10. Layer the aqua card pocket on top of the red pocket unit, aligning the lower raw edges. Topstitch through both card pockets 1" and 4½" from either side, creating two 3½" pockets. ❹

assembling the lining

1. Fuse the 12" x 9½" lightweight interfacing rectangle to the wrong side of the 12" x 9½" striped linen rectangle.

2. Layer the ticket-and-passport pocket on the linen lining, matching the raw edges along the left side and bottom. Topstitch the pocket to the lining along the right edge only by going over the previous stitching. ❺

3. To make the flap, fuse the 5" x 9½" heavyweight interfacing rectangle to the wrong side of the 5" x 9½" red geometric rectangle. Center the soft (loop) side of the 6" Velcro strip on the right side of the flap, 1" from the right edge. Topstitch the Velcro to the flap.

4. Layer the money/card pocket unit right side up on the lining unit. Layer the flap right side *down* on the money/card pocket unit, aligning all outer raw edges. Stitch. Press the seam allowances toward the flap. ❻

---

❸ Fold
2"
Topstitch.
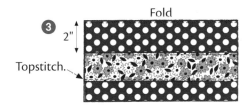

❹
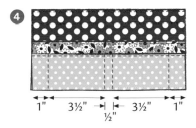
1" 3½" 3½" 1"
½"

❺
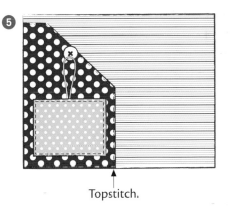
Topstitch.

❻

assembling the wallet

1. To make the wallet exterior, fuse the 15" x 9½" heavyweight interfacing rectangle to the wrong side of the 15" x 9½" airplane-and-plaid print rectangle. Layer the wallet exterior *facedown* on your work surface and the lining panel faceup, aligning all raw edges. Fold the wallet shut, marking where the Velcro hits the exterior of the wallet. Pin the stiff (hook) side of the Velcro to the exterior and fold the wallet closed again to test the placement. Once you're satisfied, unfold the wallet exterior and lining and topstitch the Velcro to the wallet exterior only.

2. To make the wrist strap, fold the 3" x 15" airplane-and-plaid print strip in half lengthwise, wrong sides together, and press. Open the strip and turn the raw edges in to meet the fold. Refold, enclosing the raw edges, and press. Topstitch ⅛" from each edge. ❼

3. Fold the wrist strap in half, matching the raw edges. Center it on the aqua polka-dot card pocket and pin. ❽

4. With right sides together and raw edges aligned, pin the lining panel to the wallet exterior. Fold down and pin the top edge of the ticket pocket if you're worried it will be caught in the seam allowance.

5. Using a *scant* ½" seam allowance, sew around the perimeter of the wallet, leaving a 4" gap on the long edge of the flap. Backstitch at the beginning and end of the seam and over the wrist strap for added strength.

6. Clip the corners and turn the wallet right side out through the gap. The wallet will be stiff, so work carefully. Roll the seams and press, being careful to avoid the button and the Velcro. Refer to "Finishing Stitches" (page 106) to close the gap.

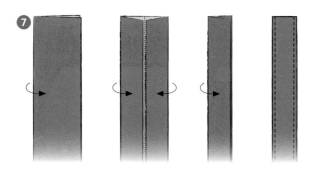

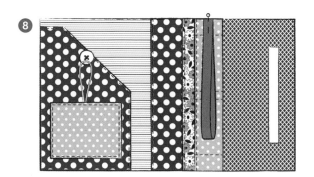

dogwood blossom
KNITTING NEEDLE CASE

This pretty case has pockets for 16 sets of double-pointed knitting needles up to 7" long, four sets of circular knitting needles, and there's even a smart little zippy pouch for notions built right in. Now you'll always have the right-sized needles on hand. This case would also be perfect for crochet hooks or colored pencils, making it a great gift for your favorite crafter.

Designed and sewn by
Adrienne Smitke

Finished Size: 6" x 10" when folded

materials
Yardage is based on 42"-wide fabric.

1 yard of teal floral print for exterior, interior flap, and binding

¾ yard of aqua herringbone print for case lining

½ yard of teal polka-dot fabric for needle pockets and zippy pouch exterior

½ yard of aqua-and-white print for needle pockets and zippy pouch lining

½ yard of fusible batting

1 yard of 1½"-wide brown woven ribbon

Painter's tape or removable fabric marker

7" zipper

cutting
From the teal floral print, cut:
1 rectangle, 12¾" x 10"
1 rectangle, 6¾" x 10"
1 rectangle, 12¾" x 14½"
2 strips, 2½" x 42"

From the teal polka-dot fabric, cut:
4 rectangles, 7" x 10½"
1 rectangle, 1¾" x 8¼"
1 rectangle, 3¾" x 8¼"
1 rectangle, 5½" x 8¼"

From the aqua herringbone print, cut:
2 rectangles, 7" x 10"
1 rectangle, 6¾" x 10"

From the aqua-and-white print, cut:
4 rectangles, 7" x 5¾"
1 rectangle, 1¾" x 8¼"
1 rectangle, 3¾" x 8¼"
1 rectangle, 5½" x 8¼"

From the fusible batting, cut:
1 rectangle, 18½" x 10"

From the brown ribbon, cut:
2 pieces, 18" long

making the case exterior

Use ½" seam allowances unless otherwise indicated.

1. Pin the 12¾" x 10" and 6¾" x 10" teal floral rectangles right sides together along their 10" sides. Find the center of this edge and insert a piece of the ribbon between the two pieces of fabric, aligning the raw edges. Sew the pieces, backstitching over the ribbon for strength. Press the seam allowances open. ❶

2. Following the manufacturer's instructions, fuse the batting rectangle to the wrong side of the unit made in step 1. Set aside.

making the pockets

1. Fold each of the 7" x 10½" teal polka-dot rectangles in half, right sides together, so they measure 7" x 5¼". Sew the long raw edges opposite the fold on each piece.

2. Finger-press the seam allowances open, turn the pockets right side out, roll the seams (page 104), and press flat. Topstitch a scant ⅛" from the fold on each pocket.

3. Layer a polka-dot pocket on a 7" x 10" herring-bone print rectangle, right side up, so the pocket seam is 2¼" from the lower edge of the rectangle. Topstitch the pocket to the lining a scant ⅛" from the bottom seam, backstitching at the beginning and end. Make two. ❷

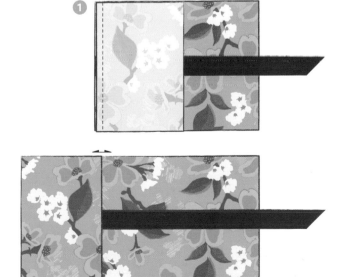

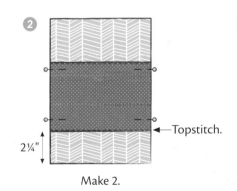

2¼"

←—Topstitch.

Make 2.

4. Pin a second polka-dot pocket on top of the first so the pocket seam is ¾" from the lower edge of the rectangle. Topstitch the pocket to the lining a scant ⅛" from the bottom seam, backstitching at the beginning and end. Make two.

5. To divide the pockets, use painter's tape or a removable marking tool to mark both sets of pockets as shown. Topstitch on the marked lines, backstitching at the beginning and end. ③

6. Pair two 7" x 5¾" aqua-and-white rectangles right sides together. Using a removable marking tool, mark ½" from the upper-left corner and 2" from the upper-right corner. Connect the marks and stitch on the line. Trim ½" beyond the seam. Make one and one reversed. ④

7. Press the seam allowances open, turn the pockets right side out, roll the seams, and press flat. Topstitch a scant ⅛" from the angled edges.

8. Pin the aqua-and-white pockets on top of the polka-dot pocket units made in steps 3 and 4,

aligning the bottom raw edges. Mark the center line of each pocket. Topstitch on the marked lines, backstitching at the beginning and end.

9. Trim *only the unit on the right* to 6¾" wide. ⑤

10. With right sides together, pin the two pocket units along the center edges. Stitch. Press the seam allowances open.

making the zippy pouch

1. Align the zipper, right side up, along the upper edge of a 1¾" x 8¼" aqua-and-white rectangle, also right side up. Align a 1¾" x 8¼" polka-dot rectangle, *wrong side up*, over the zipper and the lining. Pin. ⑥

2. Using a zipper foot and a ¼" seam allowance, sew through all layers. Move the zipper pull as needed to make stitching along the zipper easier. Press the fabrics away from the zipper using low heat and the point of your iron.

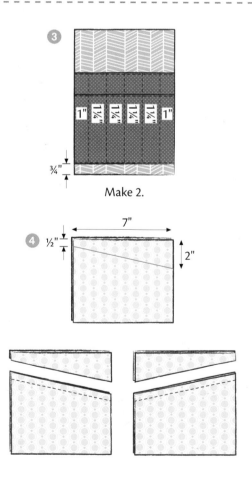

③

1" ¼" 1¼" ¼" 1¼" ¼" 1"

¾"

Make 2.

④ ½"

7"

2"

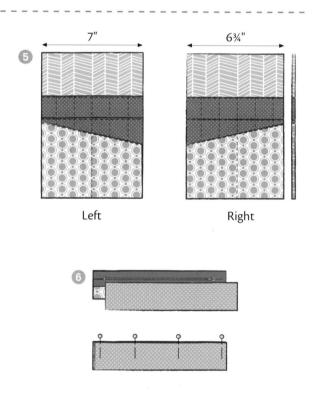

⑤

7"

6¾"

Left

Right

⑥

3. Repeat steps 1 and 2 with the 3¾" x 8¼" rectangles on the other side of the zipper.

4. Topstitch a scant ⅛" from the seams on either side of the zipper. **7**

5. Layer the 5½" x 8¼" aqua-and-white rectangle, right side up, the zipper unit you just sewed, also right side up, and the 5½" x 8¼" polka-dot rectangle, *wrong side up*, as shown, aligning the raw edges. Stitch around the sides and top of the pouch, leaving the bottom open for turning. **8**

6. Clip the corners, turn the pouch right side out, roll the seams, and press, being careful to avoid the zipper.

assembling the case

1. Center the zipper pouch, right side up, along the edge of the 6¾" x 10" herringbone rectangle, also right side up. Pin. **9**

2. Right sides together and raw edges aligned, stitch the unit made in the previous step to the left edge of the pocket unit. Press the seam allowances open. **10**

3. To make the flap, fold the 12¾" x 14½" teal floral rectangle in half, right sides together, so it measures 12¾" x 7¼". Stitch both short sides. Clip the corners, turn right side out, roll the seams, and press. Topstitch a scant ⅛" from the fold.

4. Layer the case exterior and lining panel *wrong sides together*, with the batting sandwiched in between. Center the remaining piece of ribbon on the left edge of the lining panel. Pin the flap so its top raw edges match those of the lining, and the left edge matches the seam of the zippy pouch. Pin the entire unit with safety pins. Using a long stitch, baste the perimeter a scant ¼" from the edges, backstitching on either side of the ribbon. **11**

5. Refer to "Hand-Stitched Binding" (page 108) to prepare the binding strip and attach it to the case; hand stitch the edge.

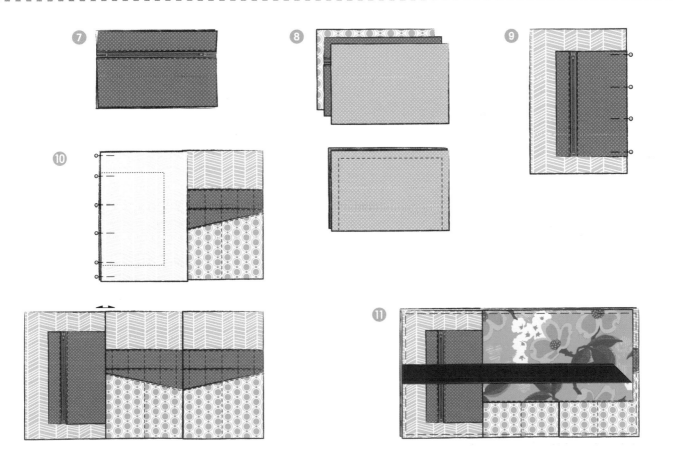

woodland SEWING SET

Bring the forest into your sewing space with this charming trio of accessories. Simple construction and techniques such as embroidery, hand stitching, and free-motion stitching make the pieces fun to sew. You'll want to employ these woodland characters to keep you company while you craft. Make just one or make the whole set.

Needle book and pouch designed and sewn by Cassie Barden; pincushion designed and sewn by Adrienne Smitke

tree stump NEEDLE BOOK

Finished Size: 3" x 3½"

materials

4" x 8" piece of dark brown felt for tree stump

1" x 3" piece of light brown felt for inner tree stump

6" x 7" piece of light green felt for leaf pages

5" square of tear-away stabilizer

Acid-free glue stick

cutting

Referring to "Making Templates and Transferring Designs" (page 104), use the freezer-paper technique and the templates on page 82 to cut out the pieces.

From the dark brown felt, cut:
1 tree stump

From the light brown felt, cut:
1 inner tree stump

From the light green felt, cut:
2 leaf pages

making the needle book

The organic stitching on the front of the book cover is a fun, low-commitment way to play with free-motion stitching, whether the technique is new to you or not. A darning foot is helpful.

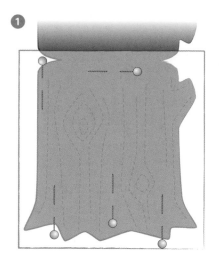

1. Transfer the tree stump stitching design to the stabilizer and pin it to the front of the book cover.

2. Thread your machine with a top thread darker than the brown felt and a bobbin thread that matches the felt. Lower the feed dogs. Test the thread tension with felt scraps before beginning. Free-motion stitch along the lines, taking two or three tiny stitches at the beginning and end of each line to secure the thread. **1**

3. Remove the stabilizer and snip the loose threads.

4. Using a swipe of glue stick, attach the inner tree stump to the front of the book cover. Alternately, use a few small, very thin pins to keep the piece from shifting. Free-motion stitch a spiral to suggest tree rings. **2**

5. Center the two leaf pages on the inside of the tree stump and pin. Stitch three times across the spine through all layers. **3**

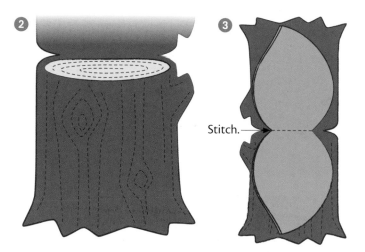

Stitch.

---

petunia hedgehog PINCUSHION

Finished Size: 5¼" x 3¼"

materials

10" x 10" piece of dark brown felt for body

3" x 6" piece of light brown felt for face

Scraps of light pink, dark pink, and green felt for flowers

Matching embroidery floss for hedgehog body

Yellow embroidery floss for flower center

Polyester or scraps of cotton batting for stuffing

Three ball-head straight pins for eyes and nose

cutting

Referring to "Making Templates and Transferring Designs" (page 104), use the freezer-paper technique and the template patterns on page 83 to cut out the pieces.

From the dark brown felt, cut:

2 hedgehog bodies

1 hedgehog base

From the light brown felt, cut:

2 hedgehog faces

From the green felt, cut:

2 large leaves

2 small leaves

From the pink felt, cut:

1 outer flower

1 inner flower

1 flower center

making the hedgehog

1. Overlap a dark brown hedgehog body ¼" on a light brown face. Using three strands of matching embroidery floss and a blanket stitch (page 106), hand stitch the body to the head. Make one and one reversed. **1**

2. Pin the two completed pieces wrong sides together, matching the raw edges. Starting at the base of the spikes, blanket stitch around the top of the hedgehog body. When you get to the face, knot the floss and hide the tail between the two layers. Change floss to a matching color and continue stitching around the face. **2**

3. Referring to the photo, attach the leaves to the side of the hedgehog. Stack the outer flower, inner flower, and flower center and attach using French knots (page 106).

4. Using the blunt end of a paintbrush or a chopstick, gently stuff the face and each of the spikes until the body is almost full but not overstuffed.

5. Fold the hedgehog base in half, finger-pressing a lengthwise crease. Use the crease to match the narrower end of the base to the face seam, and the wider end to the spike seam. Pin. Blanket stitch the base to the hedgehog. When you get 1" from the beginning, finish stuffing until you're satisfied with the shape. Close the remaining gap, knot the embroidery floss, and hide the tail inside.

6. Push two straight pins into the face for the eyes and one in the end of the snout for the nose.

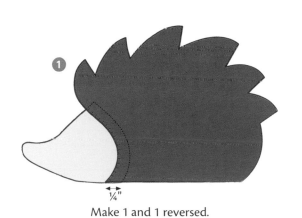

1

¼"

Make 1 and 1 reversed.

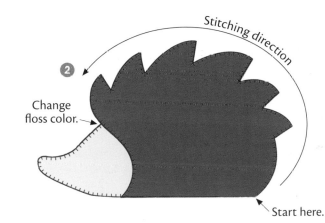

2

Stitching direction

Change floss color.

Start here.

woodland notions POUCH

Finished Size: 7½" x 5"

materials

Yardage is based on 42"-wide fabric.

⅓ yard of cotton canvas print for pouch exterior

⅓ yard of leaf print for lining

3" x 6" scrap of red polka-dot fabric for zipper tabs

⅓ yard of 20"-wide medium-weight fusible interfacing

3" length of ribbon for side tab

6" length of narrow ribbon for zipper pull

7" zipper

cutting

From the canvas print, cut:
2 rectangles, 8" x 7"

From the leaf print, cut:
2 rectangles, 8" x 7"

From the red polka-dot fabric, cut:
2 rectangles, 1" x 2½"

From the interfacing, cut:
2 rectangles, 8" x 7"

making the pouch

Use ¼" seam allowances.

1. Fold each 1" x 2½" polka-dot tab in half crosswise, wrong sides together, and press. Open one tab and align it, wrong side up, with the end of the zipper tape. Pin. Stitch on the fold twice, going over the zipper teeth carefully; see "Stitching Across a Zipper" (page 57). ❶

2. Fold the tab right side up at the stitching and topstitch a scant ⅛" from the fold. Trim the zipper end approximately ½" from the tab fold. Repeat for the other end of the zipper, moving the zipper pull a few inches out of the way. ❷

3. Following the manufacturer's instructions, fuse the interfacing rectangles to the wrong sides of the cotton canvas rectangles. Align the zipper, right side up, along the top edge of a lining piece, also right side up. Align the cotton canvas rectangle, *wrong side up*, over the zipper and the lining. Pin. Using a zipper foot and a ¼" seam allowance, sew through all layers. Move the zipper pull as needed to make stitching along the zipper easier. ❸

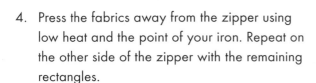

4. Press the fabrics away from the zipper using low heat and the point of your iron. Repeat on the other side of the zipper with the remaining rectangles.

5. Topstitch through all layers a scant ⅛" from the seams on either side of the zipper. ❹

6. Unzip the zipper halfway. (You'll turn the bag right side out through the open zipper, so don't forget this step!) Bring the canvas pieces right sides together and the lining pieces right sides together, matching the raw edges and letting the zipper ends fold over on themselves, with the zipper teeth toward the cotton canvas rather the lining. (The zipper teeth will face upward once the finished bag is turned right side out.) Fold the ribbon tab in half and slip it between the two outer pieces along one side as shown, aligning the raw edges. ❺

7. Sew around the perimeter, leaving a 3" gap in the lining on one side. Go slowly and carefully over the bulky zipper ends. Finger-press the seams open. ❻

8. To box the first lining corner, flatten the lining so the bottom and side seams align. Mark a stitching line 1¼" from the corner point and perpendicular to the seam. Sew along the marked line twice. Trim the corner ¼" from the stitching. Repeat on the remaining corner. ❼

9. Turn the pouch right side out through the gap and the open zipper. Box the outside corners as in step 8, but do not trim; instead, tack each corner to the side of the pouch by stitching an X with embroidery floss. Take a few tiny stitches in the seam allowance to secure. ❽

10. Tie a bit of narrow ribbon to the zipper to create a decorative zipper pull.

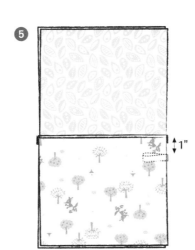

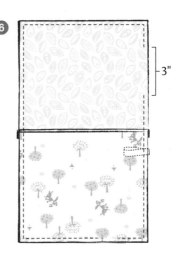

3"

1"

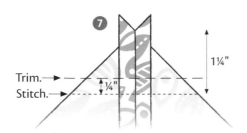

Trim.
Stitch.
¼"
1¼"

Tack.

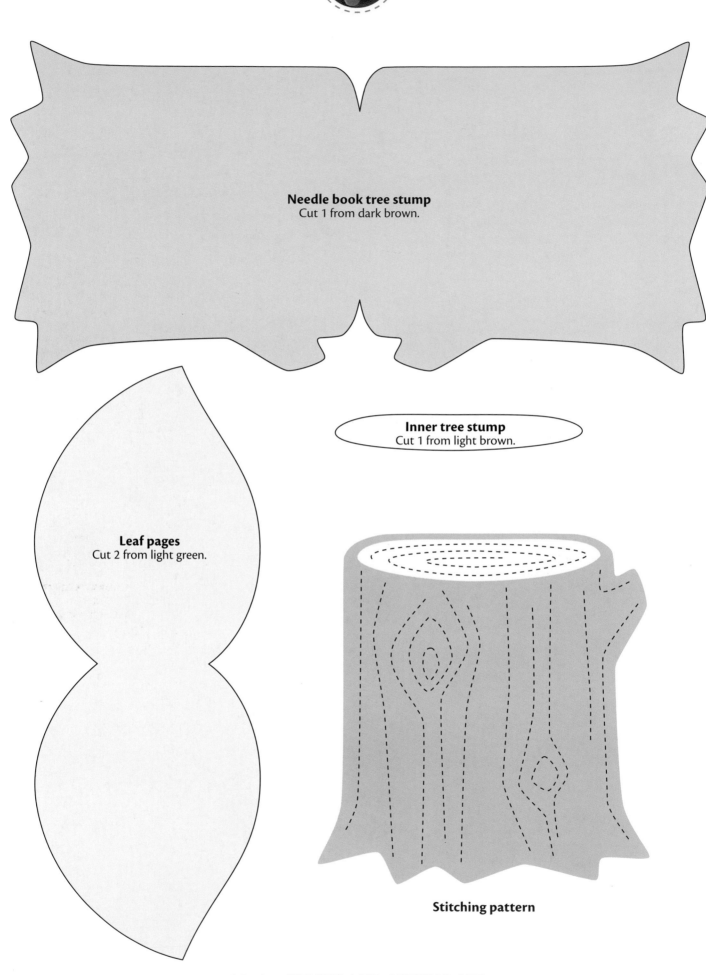

Needle book tree stump
Cut 1 from dark brown.

Inner tree stump
Cut 1 from light brown.

Leaf pages
Cut 2 from light green.

Stitching pattern

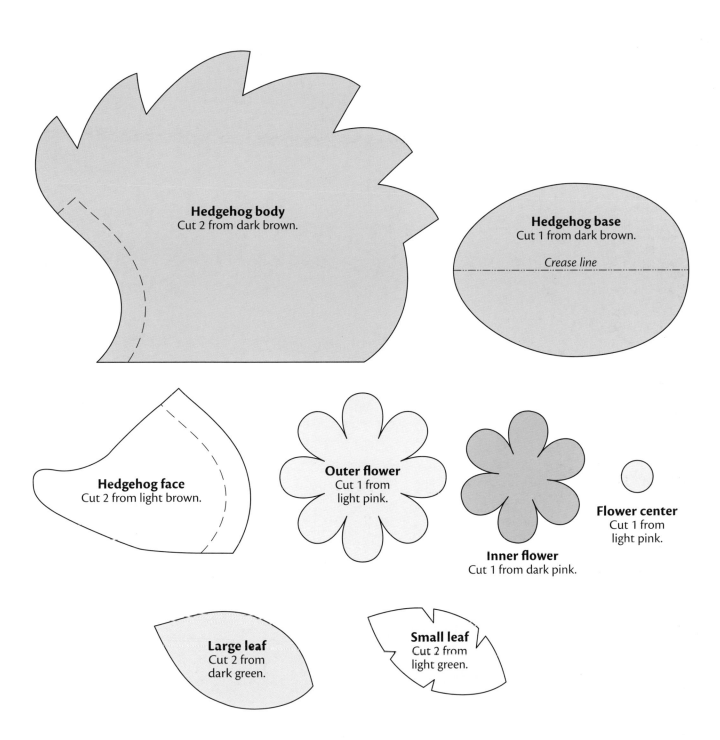

Hedgehog body
Cut 2 from dark brown.

Hedgehog base
Cut 1 from dark brown.

Crease line

Hedgehog face
Cut 2 from light brown.

Outer flower
Cut 1 from
light pink.

Inner flower
Cut 1 from dark pink.

Flower center
Cut 1 from
light pink.

Large leaf
Cut 2 from
dark green.

Small leaf
Cut 2 from
light green.

in the clouds BABY QUILT

Clouds are one of my favorite design motifs, so when I was thinking of ways to incorporate them into a baby quilt, I imagined strings of pennants fluttering in the breeze above baby's head. This is a super-fast, easy quilt, making it perfect for gift giving. I used a rainbow of tone-on-tone prints for the pennants, but you can use any color scheme to match a nursery decor. Everything except the rickrack is fused and then appliquéd by machine onto a single width of fabric, so there's no piecing whatsoever.

Designed and sewn
by Cassie Barden

Finished Size: 36" x 50"

materials

Yardage is based on 42"-wide fabric.

1⅝ yards of blue fabric for background

½ yard of white fabric for clouds

Scraps (at least 12" x 12") of 16 assorted prints for pennants and pieced binding

1 yard of 17"-wide paper-backed fusible web

Two packages (130" total) of medium rickrack for pennant string

1⅔ yards of fabric for backing

44" x 58" piece of batting

making the quilt

1. Using the template patterns on page 87–89, trace one cloud for each pattern piece (one cloud and one cloud reversed for piece D) onto the paper side of the fusible web. Trace 16 pennants onto the paper side of the fusible web. Refer to "Appliqué" (page 105) to finish preparing your appliqués.

2. Trim the background fabric to 36" x 50".

3. Arrange the clouds and pennants as shown, stepping back periodically to make sure you're happy with the placement. I like to arrange the clouds and pennants at the same time, although you'll have to remove some pennants to stitch the clouds. Drape string as a guide to "hang" the pennants at the correct angle. Once satisfied, pin all pieces except the

pennants that will be overlapping clouds. Snap a photo of the quilt so it's easy to position these pennants once the clouds are stitched. ①

4. Peel the paper backing from the cloud and pennant pieces and fuse them to the background, following the manufacturer's instructions. Use a blanket stitch to machine appliqué the pieces.

5. Replace the temporarily removed pennants and fuse them to the background. Using top thread to match each pennant and a blanket stitch, machine appliqué the pennants.

6. Refer to "Quiltmaking Basics" (page 108) to prepare your finished quilt top for quilting. You might also consider taking your quilt to a professional long-arm or hand quilter.

7. Once quilted, pin the rickrack so it covers the top edges and corners of the pennants. Stitch down the middle to secure it to the quilt.

I sewed the rickrack down last because I wanted it to be on top of everything else, but you can add it before quilting if desired. ②

8. Prepare the binding by cutting random-length 2½"-wide strips from your pennant scraps. For a small quilt like this, strips 6" to 12" long work well. Sew the strips end to end until you have one strip at least 182" long. Referring to "Binding" (page 108), finish preparing the binding strip and bind the quilt.

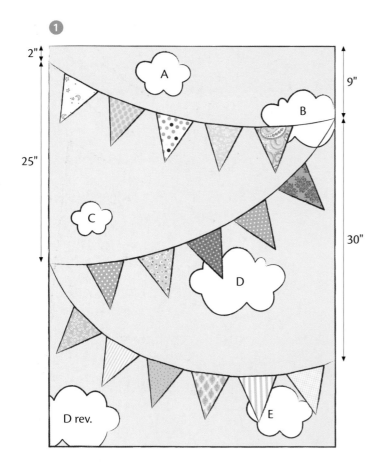

Cloud C
Cut 1.

Cloud A
Cut 1.

Cloud E
Cut 1.

Cloud patterns are reversed
for fusible appliqué.

Pennant
Cut 16.

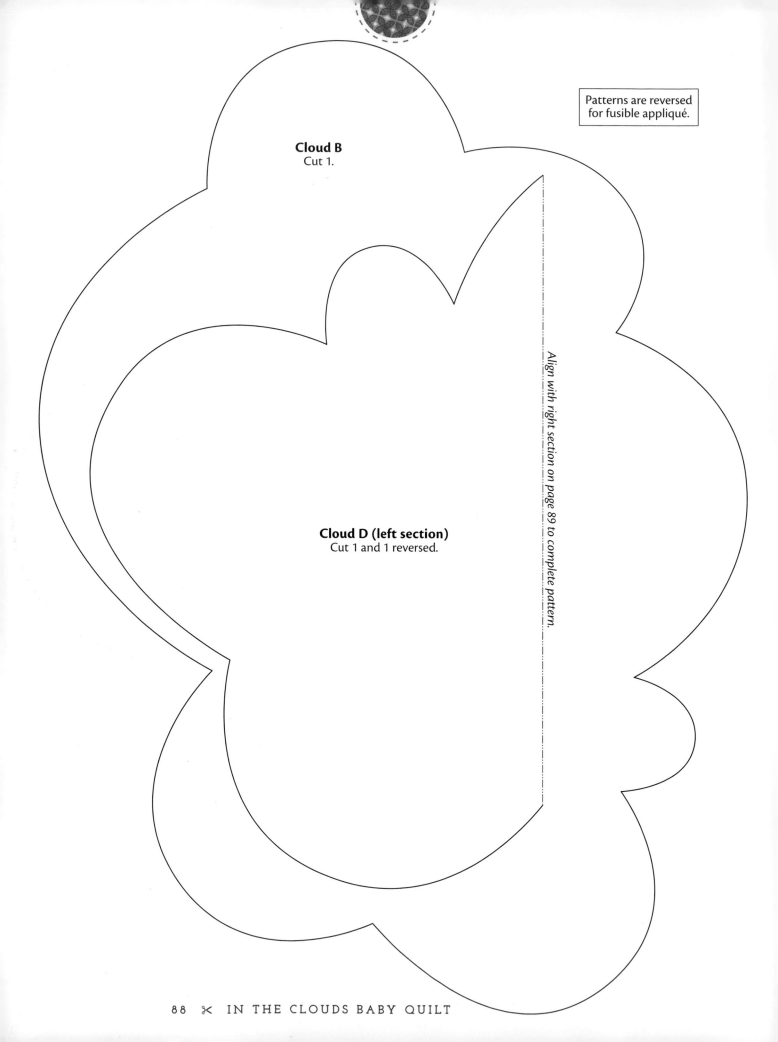

Cloud B
Cut 1.

Cloud D (left section)
Cut 1 and 1 reversed.

Align with right section on page 89 to complete pattern.

Cloud D (right section)

Align with left section on page 88 to complete pattern.

fenn the JACKALOPE

Fenn left the Southwest deserts of the United States as a young jackalope, itching to see the world. He has photographed endangered camels on the steppe of Mongolia and walked the lava fields of Iceland, sampled satay on the lively streets of Kuala Lampur and dined on ceviche in Peru. After any adventure, he prefers to sit in a café with a bit of cocoa, a pastry, and a good book. Fenn currently resides with his flatmate (a narwhal) in Seattle, where he writes short fiction, and where the many coffee shops keep him cozy throughout the year.

Designed and sewn
by Cassie Barden

Finished Size: 15" x 23" (including ears)

materials

Yardage is based on 42"-wide fabric.

⅓ yard of wool or wool-blend fabric for jackalope

10" x 10" square of cotton print for inner ears

6" x 6" square of brown felt for antlers

1" x 14" strip of purple felt for scarf

Tear-away stabilizer

Black embroidery floss

Brown embroidery floss to match felt

One 14-ounce bag of cotton or polyester stuffing

cutting

Referring to "Making Templates and Transferring Designs" (page 104), use the freezer-paper technique and the templates on pages 94–96 to cut out the pieces.

From the wool, cut:
2 jackalope bodies

2 arms

2 arms reversed

2 ears

From the cotton print, cut:
2 ears

From the brown felt, cut:
4 antlers

From the purple felt, cut:
1 strip, 1" x 16"

making the jackalope

Use ½" seam allowances unless otherwise indicated.

1. To prepare the antlers, whipstitch (page 106) two antler pieces together, starting on the pronged edge. Once you get a few stitches around the top, gently stuff the points. **1**

2. Continue taking several stitches and stuffing the antler as you work toward the bottom. Leave the bottom of the antler open and tie off your thread so it's hidden in the seam allowance. Finish stuffing the antler, leaving approximately ½" for the seam allowance. Repeat for the second antler.

3. To prepare the ears, sew one wool and one cotton ear right sides together around the curved edges, leaving the bottom open. Clip the points and curves, turn right side out, and press.

4. Fold each ear on the dashed lines shown on the pattern and pin. Baste ¼" from the raw edges. **2**

5. To prepare the arms, sew two arm pieces right sides together around the curved edges, leaving the straight edge (the "shoulder") open. Clip the curves, turn right side out, and press. Fill the arm with stuffing, leaving ½" at the shoulder for the seam allowance. Repeat for the second arm.

6. Using three strands of black embroidery floss and tear-away stabilizer, stitch the belly button and face details onto the front body. I used a backstitch for the eyes and mouth, a stem stitch to border the nose, and a satin stitch to fill in the nose. (See "Embroidery" on page 106.)

7. The next two steps are a bit tricky, but pin carefully and sew slowly, and you'll be successful. Layer all pieces as shown, matching the raw edges. Start with the back of the jackalope body, right side facing up. Lay the ears, with the inner piece of each ear facing up, on the head, followed by the antlers. Lay the arms on the chest. Last, lay the front body piece *right side down* on top of everything and pin the perimeter. **3**

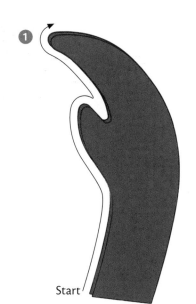

Start

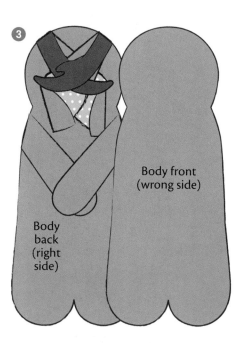

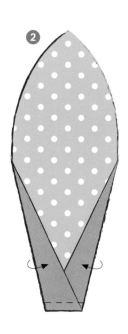

Body front (wrong side)

Body back (right side)

8. Sew around the perimeter, leaving a 4" gap along one side, between an arm and a leg. Backstitch at the beginning and end. Clip the curves around the feet and head, and between the legs. **4**

9. Gently turn right side out through the gap. Fill the head and body with stuffing and sew the gap closed using a ladder stitch (page 107).

10. Trim 5" off the felt strip and clip one end to create fringe. Using a few small hand stitches, secure the other end to Fenn's chest, at the neck. Wrap the remainder of the strip around the neck, covering the first strip. Trim so the ends meet at the back of the neck and hand stitch. **5**

Good Stuff

For best results, stuff gently using small bits of stuffing at a time. Do not shove the stuffing, or you'll create lumps. For small areas use a slim, blunt object (like the end of a paintbrush, knitting needle, or chopstick) to ease bits of stuffing into the crevices and points. I like to stuff the doll a little firmer than I think I need, because the stuffing compresses a bit when you're done.

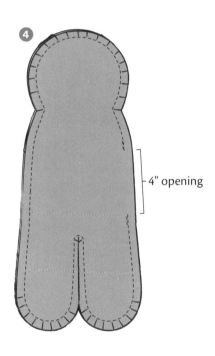

4" opening

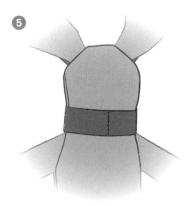

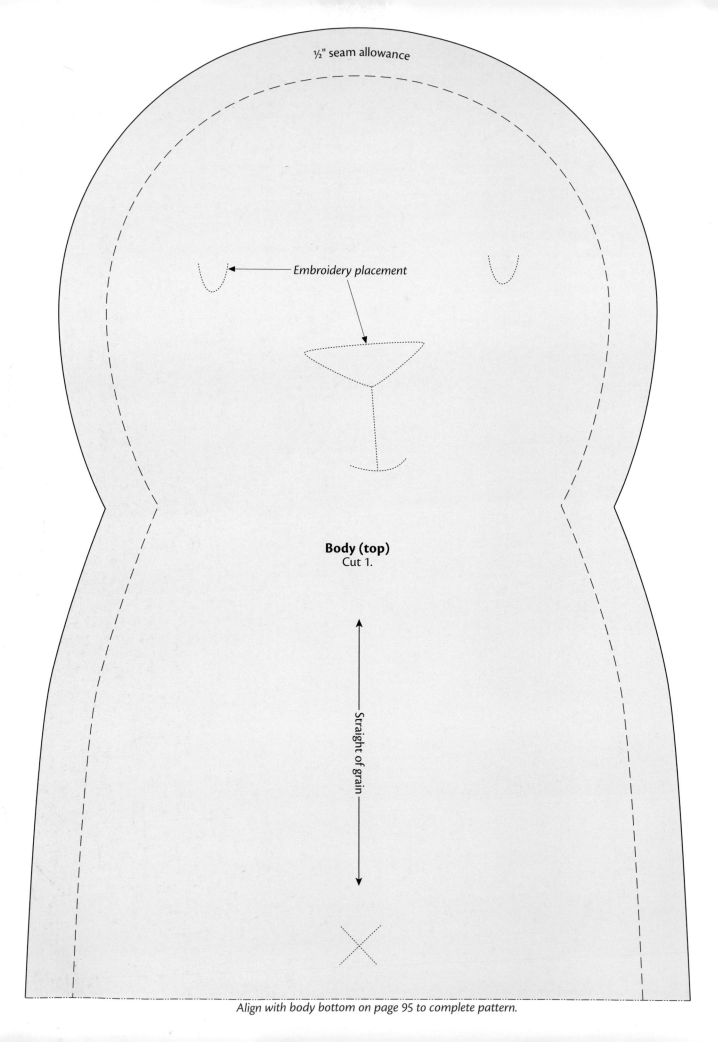

½" seam allowance

Embroidery placement

Body (top)
Cut 1.

Straight of grain

Align with body bottom on page 95 to complete pattern.

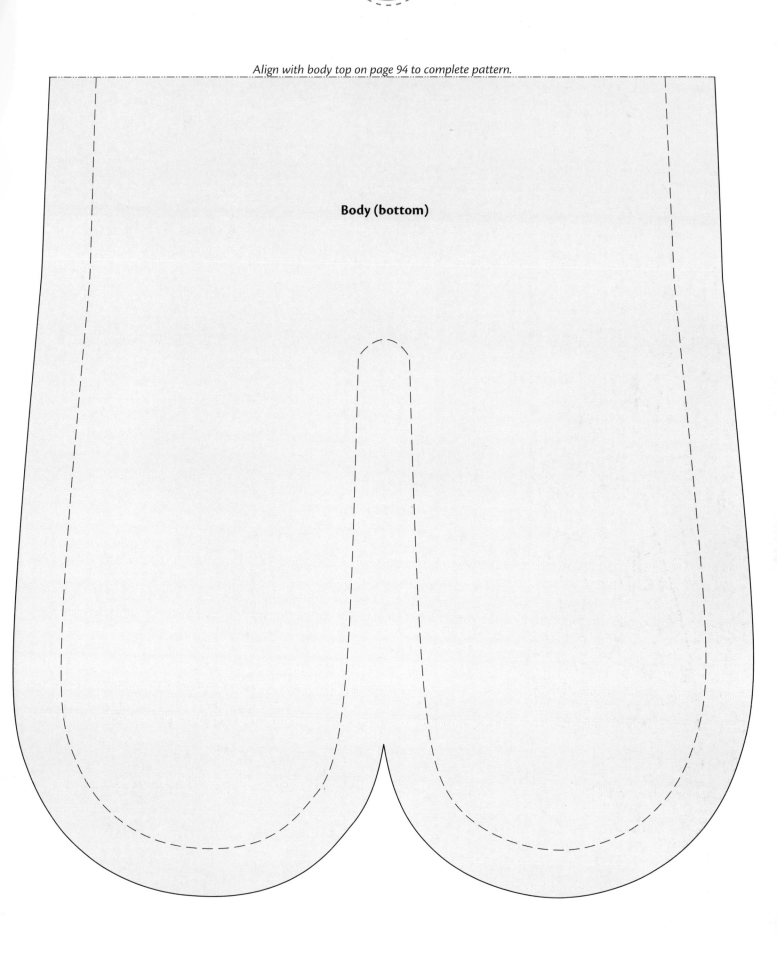

Align with body top on page 94 to complete pattern.

Body (bottom)

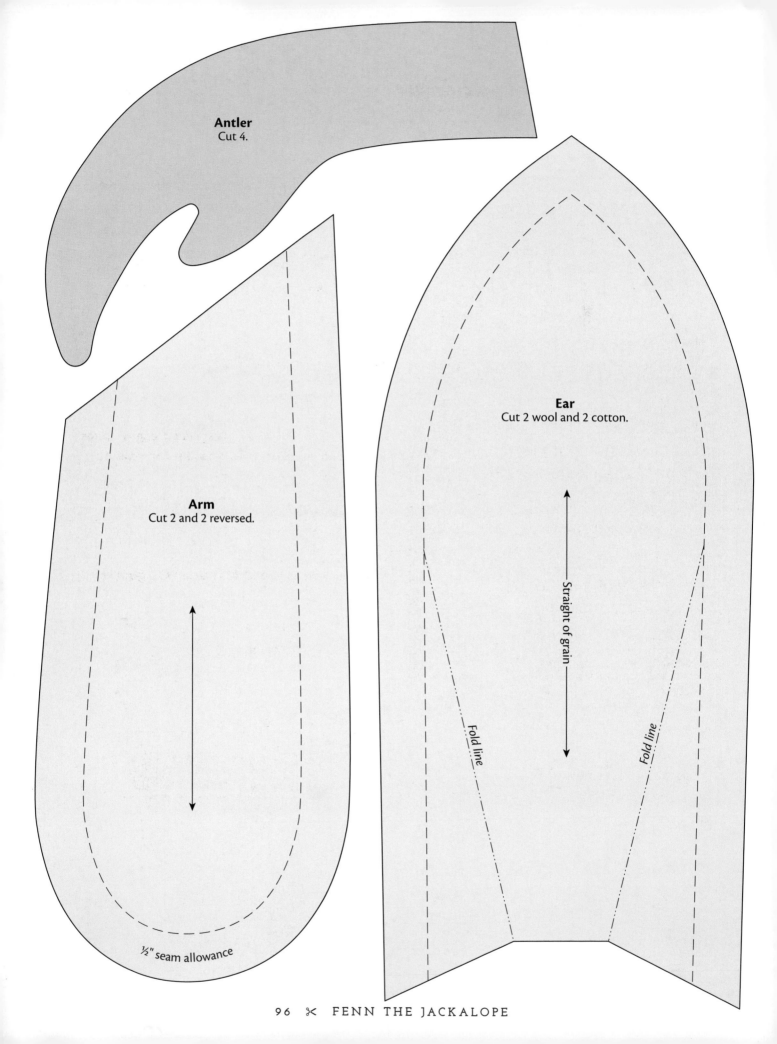

Antler
Cut 4.

Arm
Cut 2 and 2 reversed.

½" seam allowance

Ear
Cut 2 wool and 2 cotton.

Straight of grain

Fold line

Fold line

weird science LAP QUILT

This modular lap quilt is the perfect size for snuggling under while watching your favorite '80s movie. Hexagons were traditionally hand sewn or paper pieced, but this quilt takes advantage of a half hexagon template, which allows you to machine sew the pieces without the hassle of inset seams. The organic design of this quilt is perfect for showcasing a collection of favorite fabrics—and your own creativity—because the hexagons can be arranged in an endless number of patterns.

Designed and pieced by
Adrienne Smitke;
hand quilted by Cathy Valentine

Finished Size: 63" x 64"

materials

Yardage is based on 42"-wide fabric.

2½ yards of white solid fabric for background and binding

1½ yards *total* of assorted blue and green solids for hexagons

4 yards of fabric for backing

71" x 72" piece of batting

Template plastic

cutting

Referring to "Making Templates and Transferring Designs" (page 104), use the plastic template technique and the templates on page 100 to cut out the pieces.

From the white fabric, cut:
15 strips, 4½" x 42"; cut into:

    66 half hexagons

    16 regular setting triangles and 16 reversed triangles ❶
7 strips, 2½" x 42"

From the assorted blue and green solids, cut:
40 matching pairs of half hexagons

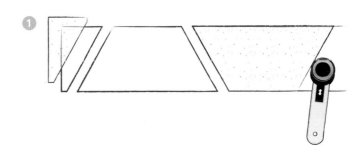

❶

It's All About Options

Don't get too caught up trying to match the exact fabrics in my quilt. Instead, make this quilt your own by using colors you like best. Not sure where to begin? Here are some other fabric options.

- **Limited palette.** Consult your color wheel. Try using just warm or just cool colors. Or use one of these color-theory combinations: analogous colors, complementary colors, or split complementary colors.

- **Super scrappy.** For a fantastic stash-buster quilt, you'll need scraps at least 10" square to cut two half hexagons from each. To use the layout of the quilt above, you'll also need a total of 40 pairs of half hexagons, plus the background pieces from the cutting list.

- **Layer cakes.** Use one white solid Layer Cake (a collection of precut 10" squares) and one assorted Layer Cake, plus ⅝ yard of fabric for binding.

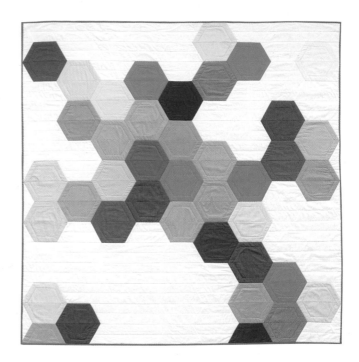

assembling the quilt

Use ¼" seam allowances.

1. Referring to the illustration below, lay out the half hexagons and setting triangles, keeping the half hexagons in matched pairs. ②

2. Sew the half hexagon pieces together in horizontal rows, offsetting them ¼" as shown. Press the seam allowances toward the darker fabrics. ③

3. Sew a white setting triangle to each end of each row, offsetting the piece ¼". ④

4. Sew the rows together, pressing the seam allowances in one direction.

5. Refer to "Quiltmaking Basics" (page 108) to finish and bind your quilt. You might also consider having your quilt professionally machine or hand quilted (as I did).

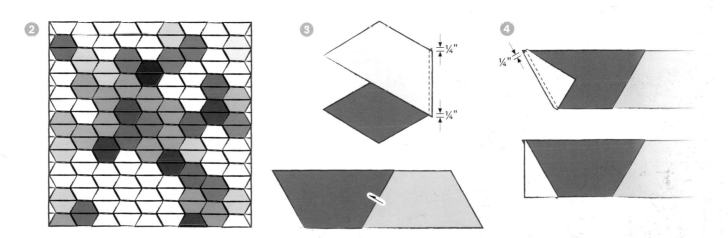

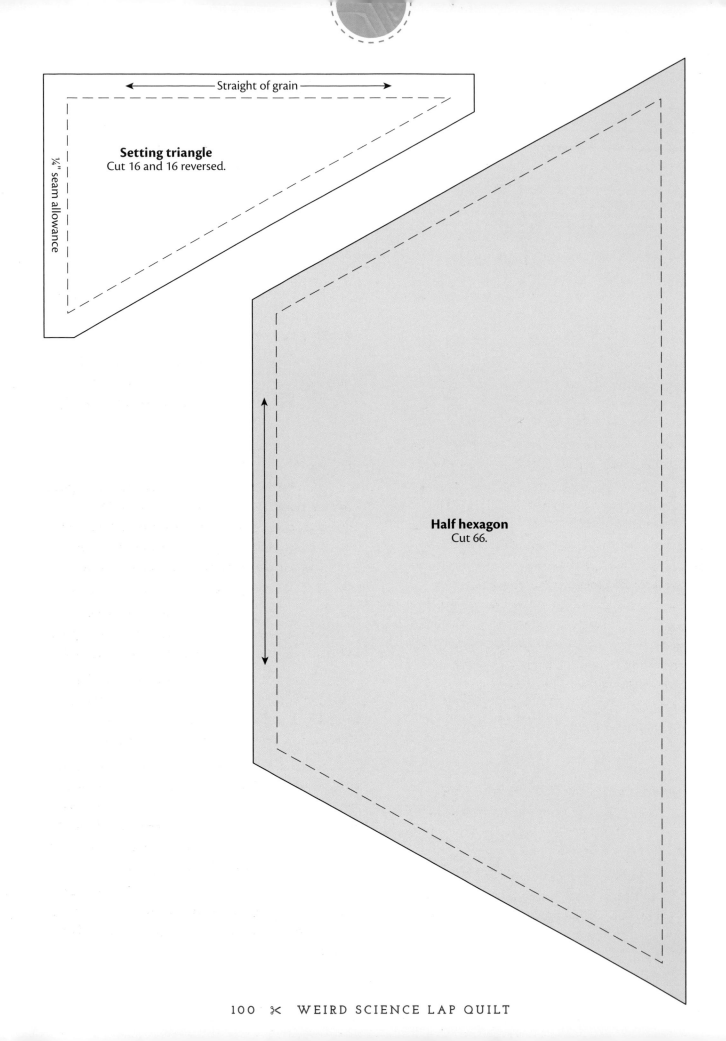

Setting triangle
Cut 16 and 16 reversed.

Straight of grain

¼" seam allowance

Half hexagon
Cut 66.

GENERAL INSTRUCTIONS

Whether you're an experienced sewist or a complete rookie, every project begins here, with the basics. Here's what you'll need to get started and to ensure that your sewing is successful and fun.

TOOLS of the trade

Having the right tools is the first step toward successful sewing. If you've already got some sewing experience, you may have many of the tools listed below. Although you don't need all of these tools to begin, you'll get the most out of your skills if you know what's available.

me, myself, and my machine

Your sewing machine is your most important tool, and you should treat it as such. Keeping your machine cleaned and serviced will go a long way toward better performance and a better finished product. Whether you own a workhorse 1970s-era Singer inherited from your mother (like Adrienne), or a fancy-pants new Bernina (like Cassie), most general-purpose sewing machines will work for the projects in this book. Make sure your machine can backstitch, as that is essential, and if you're unsure how your machine will react to a new material or technique, test it on a swatch first. No matter what kind of machine you have, take the time to read the manual, or, if you really want to get to know your machine, take a sewing class. Even if you've been sewing for years, you're sure to learn something new!

machine needles

Become familiar with the different kinds of machine needles and when to use each. Change your needle regularly or at the start of each new project. Here are the most common machine needles we use.

Universal needles work with most fabrics. The tip is sharp enough to pierce woven fabrics but slightly rounded to allow it to push between the fibers of knit fabrics.

Sharp needles have a sharp point for stitching woven fabrics. Sharps are especially good for topstitching and other decorative stitching.

Jeans/Denim needles aren't just for sewing denim. They have a strong shaft and a sharp point that's great for sewing through lots of layers or heavyweight fabrics.

presser feet

Just as you'll use different needles for specific projects, different presser feet have their own roles. Most sewing machines come with a few different feet, but if you are new to sewing or you're using an older machine, here are some feet you'll want to have.

Standard foot. A standard presser foot is used for sewing straight stitches. It's also good for sewing zigzag or other decorative stitches because the space in the foot allows the needle to move from side to side.

Zipper foot. Like its name suggests, this foot is for sewing in a zipper, but it's also useful for making and attaching piping. The most common zipper foot is narrow, allowing you to sew close to the zipper teeth.

Walking foot. Most often used in quilting, this foot has its own set of feed dogs (the little teeth that move the fabric along) to "pull" the top layer at the same speed as the machine's feed dogs move the bottom layer. A walking foot is also useful when sewing two interfaced layers of fabric to avoid "sticking" (page 103).

Free-motion/darning foot. This foot is designed for free-motion quilting. Most darning feet have a very open design so you can see marked lines as well as your stitching.

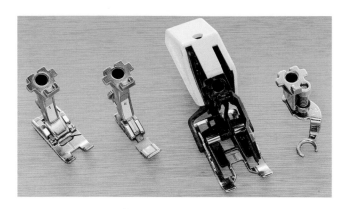

Commonly used presser feet from left to right: regular foot, zipper foot, walking foot, and free-motion quilting foot

looking sharp: cutting tools

Most of the projects in this book involve rectangular shapes and can be cut using a rotary cutter and cutting mat. If you've never tried a rotary cutter, give it a whirl—it's a great time-saving tool. Just be sure to keep your fingers away from the blade and use a self-healing mat under your fabric to protect the cutting surface.

Sometimes you'll need to mark the fabric and cut out a shape using scissors. If you're more accustomed to cutting fabric in this way, you can cut out every pattern piece in the book with scissors. There are lots of different kinds of scissors on the market, and it's worth having a few in your arsenal. These are the ones you'll find in our sewing baskets.

Scissors for fabric. These should be large and comfortable to hold. Buy them at your local fabric store—they are worth the extra cost. To keep them sharp, don't use your fabric scissors to cut anything else. As kids, we both learned that one of the worst offenses was to use Mom's sewing scissors to cut paper!

Scissors for small precision work. A pair of small, sharp scissors is useful for cutting out appliqué designs or pieces with tight curves or points. The tips on these scissors give you a lot of leverage and control when cutting small or detailed designs.

All-purpose, "el-cheapo" office scissors. These scissors are for everything else: template plastic, Velcro, paper, you name it. Save your nice fabric scissors and pick up a pack of these "kitchen scissors." You'll thank us later.

Thread snips. These small snappy scissors are perfect for snipping stray threads or getting into tight spots with their short, sharp blades. Keep a pair next to your machine for easy access.

the heat is on: pressing tools

A good-quality iron with a steam function is essential. If your iron doesn't have a steam feature, you can improvise by using a spray bottle on the mist setting. Lightly mist the fabric until just damp (don't soak it), and then press to remove wrinkles or to open a seam.

If you have the space, a full-size ironing board is worth it, but if you're short on room, look for a mini ironing board or use an insulated ironing pad that can be placed on the table or floor.

interfacing

Interfacing is a material used to stiffen, add structure to, or strengthen fabric. It comes in different forms—woven or nonwoven, fusible or sew-in. We prefer fusible, nonwoven interfacing for the projects in this book.

You'll find interfacing in various weights, typically lightweight, mediumweight, and heavyweight, but because there is no standard terminology ("sheer" in one brand may be "lightweight" in another), you'll need to use your judgment in choosing the right weight for your project.

Interfacing is inexpensive and nice to have on hand, so buy more than what's required. Store your leftover interfacing with the manufacturer's directions in a ziplock bag or plastic bin for future reference and make sure to mark the weight.

Is Interfacing Making Your Sewing "Sticky"?

Sometimes sewing two pieces of interfaced fabric makes your machine feel "sticky," as though things just aren't moving under the presser foot. Try switching to a walking foot or adjusting the tension on your machine for smoother stitching.

on pins and needles

Pins. Pinning is an important part of accurate sewing. Long, stiff, straight pins are great for all-purpose fabrics, especially for canvas or multiple layers of fabric. Smaller, thinner pins are good for areas when you don't have much room to pin or for delicate fabrics. No matter the size of the pin, glass-head pins have the advantage of not melting under your iron should you accidentally miss one. Lastly, curved safety pins are great for pinning multiple layers of fabric and batting when preparing to quilt. Look for these at quilting and fabric stores.

Needles. A standard hand-sewing needle is fine for most work. If you're having trouble getting the needle through the fabric, you may be using a needle that's too thick or has an eye that's too wide. If you're unsure which needle will work best, buy a package of assorted hand-sewing needles and experiment. For embroidery, try crewel embroidery needles. For more information on embroidery tools and techniques see "Embroidery" (page 106).

the ties that bind: thread

Use high-quality cotton thread like Superior, Aurifil, Mettler, or Gutermann, which is available at quilting, fabric, and craft stores. For piecing projects that use several different-colored fabrics, use a neutral color so you don't have to change the thread often. It's always good to have a stash of large spools of versatile neutral colors like white, cream, beige, gray, and black. For topstitching and quilting, a variety of threads are available, from solid cottons to metallics and color-changing variegated threads.

measuring tools

Rulers and other measuring tools are, of course, absolutely necessary. Besides the ubiquitous measuring tape, clear acrylic rulers in different shapes and sizes are invaluable. If you decide to use a rotary cutter, you'll need an acrylic ruler—generally used for quilting—to cut against. Even if you are marking patterns and cutting with scissors, these rulers make great straight edges. Another indispensable ruler is a sewing and knitting gauge. It's a slim, 6"-long metal ruler with a slide marker on it. It's perfect for taking small, quick measurements as you work.

making your mark

There seem to be as many marking tools as there are crafters. With any marking tool, especially the "disappearing ink" variety, always test on a scrap of fabric before committing. Here are a few of our favorite tools.

Clover white marking pen. This is a great tool for darker fabrics. The pen creates a clean white line that will take a moment to appear, but then it disappears with heat from your iron.

Clover blue water-soluble marking pen. This pen draws a bright blue line that disappears with water. It's great for use on lighter fabrics.

Chalk pencils. You'll find a wide variety of chalk pencils and chalk marking tools. Experiment to find one that brushes off easily.

Transfer paper. Our brand of choice is Saral. It comes in several colors and is available at fabric and art stores. Saral is wax-free, which means it will erase and brush off. If you plan to mark pattern lines where they could later show, test the marks just in case.

Blue painter's tape. It may seem a little odd to include tape in a list of marking tools, but painter's tape is fantastic for marking straight lines for topstitching. Painter's tape is less sticky than regular masking tape and will come off easily without leaving a residue (though you shouldn't leave the tape on for long or iron over it). Simply stitch along the edge of the tape (not through it).

techniques

A book with such a broad range of projects is bound to draw on a variety of techniques, some that you're familiar with, and some not. All are worth reviewing, no matter what your skill level.

pressing seams

You'll notice that most project instructions indicate to "press" the seam allowances. It's important to understand that pressing is not ironing. Ironing involves pushing the iron back and forth while applying pressure, which can distort seams or stretch layers of fabric. Instead, press by applying gentle pressure without moving the iron.

Another technique to achieve clean-finished seams is to "roll" them. Sometimes hard-to-iron seams look curled or puffy—as when you've attached the lining of a bag to the outer bag and turned it right side out. This is the time to literally roll the seam on a flat surface, such as an ironing board, cutting mat, or your pant leg (jeans work great), so that the top fabric rolls slightly to the inside. The more the fabric sticks to the surface, the better—if it's sliding under your hands, nothing will happen. You want the bottom fabric to "grab" the flat surface as your fingers roll the top fabric forward. It sounds confusing, but give it a try—it's worth the effort to get a wonderful finished edge.

making templates and transferring designs

Unless you are working freehand, you need a method to transfer your designs or patterns from paper to fabric. Here are several ways to go about it.

templates

Templates are perfect for designs or pattern pieces you'll use many times. Once you've created a template, simply trace around it onto the fabric with your marking tool. We recommend template plastic, a stiff translucent plastic found at quilting and craft stores, but cardboard or cardstock will work as well. You can trace designs directly onto the plastic with a

Sharpie pen, and then cut out the design with sharp scissors (just don't use your fabric scissors!). For embroidery use a water-soluble or air-soluble pen to trace your design onto the background fabric.

pattern tissue

Traditionally used in garment sewing, pattern tissue is useful for smaller pattern pieces. Simply trace the design onto the pattern tissue, pin it to your fabric, and cut along the marked lines.

paper-backed fusible web

There are several brands of paper-backed fusible web for transferring designs. See "Appliqué" (facing page) for an overview of the process, and always follow the manufacturer's instructions carefully.

freezer paper

Freezer paper, available at grocery stores, can be used for single appliqué shapes or to transfer templates to fabric, like on the yoke of the Portlander Shoulder Bag (page 18) or with Fenn the Jackalope (page 90). Freezer paper also works well for transferring designs to felt, which can be difficult to mark with typical temporary methods. Trace your *reversed* design onto the paper side of the freezer paper, roughly cut around the design, and press the plastic side onto the wrong side of your fabric with a dry iron on medium heat. Cut out your design and pull away the freezer paper.

For fusible appliqué (our appliqué technique of choice), freezer paper is wonderful in conjunction with loose fusible web like Misty Fuse. Trace your *reversed* design onto the paper side of the freezer paper and roughly cut around the design. Lay a piece of fusible web in between the plastic side of the freezer paper and the wrong side of your fabric and press. Cut around your design and pull away the freezer paper, leaving the fusible web adhered to the fabric. This is an excellent method to try if you've had bad luck with paper-backed fusible web, and some people prefer the extremely lightweight results they get with Misty Fuse.

design transfer

There are several methods for transferring embroidery designs to your background fabric.

Tear-away or water-soluble stabilizer is great if you don't want to mark on the material, or for backgrounds such as felt that are difficult to mark. Draw or trace your design onto the stabilizer first, secure it to the background, and stitch directly through it. Either gently remove the paper for tear-away stabilizer or submerge the piece in water to dissolve water-soluble stabilizer. You can also use tissue paper as tear-away stabilizer.

Carbon paper is great when you already have a printout or drawing of the design. Because it makes a somewhat permanent mark on the fabric, you'll need to cover the marked lines completely with your stitches. Layer the carbon paper and design on your fabric and use a sharp pencil to trace the design.

Marking directly on your fabric is a quick and simple method of design transfer that works great on lighter fabrics. Using a light box, a sunny window, or working freehand, trace or draw your design onto the background fabric using a water-soluble or air-soluble marking pen.

appliqué

Appliqué is one of our favorite ways to add personality to a project. Raw-edge appliqué is quick and easy, has a very gentle learning curve even for complex designs, and looks good, too!

We use two techniques for raw-edge appliqué, depending on the fabrics involved. If stitching appliqués made of quilting cottons or similar lightweight materials, our favorite method is to use paper-backed fusible web to transfer and fuse the design, and a machine stitch to appliqué the pieces to the background. Here's a basic guide to get you started:

1. Trace the *reversed* template or design onto the paper side of the fusible web. (The patterns in this book that call for fusible web are already reversed.) Roughly cut around the tracing, leaving ½" beyond the marked line. For larger shapes, also trim away the paper in the center of the design, leaving at least a ½" margin. **1**

2. Following the manufacturer's instructions, fuse the web to the wrong side of the fabric. Cut out the drawn shape on the marked line. **2**

3. Peel away the paper backing, and fuse the appliqué to the right side of your background fabric.

4. Use the machine stitch of your choice to secure the appliqué. Blanket stitch, zigzag, and satin stitch are all good options. Test on a scrap of fabric to choose the one that's best for your appliqué. **3**

For felt appliqués, draw the design directly onto the felt using a fine-point craft pen or use freezer paper (facing page) to transfer the design. Machine or hand stitch the appliqué using a running or blanket stitch (page 106).

Many machines have decorative stitches that make unique edgings on appliqué, and many hand-embroidery stitches look lovely around the edges of a felt design. For felt appliqués, decorative stitching within the shape, such as stitched veins on a leaf, can also secure the design.

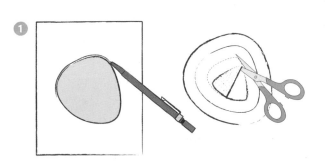

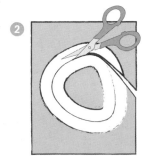

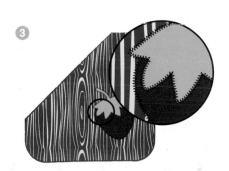

embroidery

While traditional embroidery might evoke Victorian ladies stitching elaborate floral designs or monogramming their husbands' handkerchiefs, modern embroidery can be as free-form as you like—think of embroidery as drawing with thread. It's easy and very affordable. For simple embroidery projects like those in this book, you really need only a few tools.

Embroidery hoop. An embroidery hoop is necessary when stitching on fabrics without much structure. A hoop 7" or smaller is sufficient for the projects in this book. If you get serious about embroidery, we recommend searching for a deep, high-quality hoop of solid wood. The better the hoop, the tighter it will hold your fabric, and for longer. Standard hoops at craft stores work fine, however, and are inexpensive enough that you can have a variety of sizes.

Background fabric. For the embroidery in this book, 100% linen is a good choice.

Crewel embroidery needles. These needles are designated by number, with a higher number indicating a finer needle. Size 3/8 crewel needles will accommodate three to six strands of cotton floss.

Cotton embroidery floss. A skein of floss is made up of six strands twisted together, which can be separated into individual strands for finer stitches. While it depends on personal preference as well as the design, we most often work with three or four strands at a time. **3**

finishing stitches

There are a variety of stitches you can use to complete your project. Each has its own advantages, but all the stitches below are worth learning.

Whipstitch. This hand stitch is a favorite for closing a gap in a lining. It's fast, and there's something satisfying about making tiny, regular stitches. It's not invisible, like the ladder stitch (facing page), but if you use matching thread and make very small stitches, it will fade into the project.

1. Start by burying the knot under the machine-stitched portion of the seam, just before the area you need to whipstitch.

2. Make a small, diagonal stitch across the seam, insert the needle into the back, and bring it through the front at the same point. Repeat this motion by making another diagonal stitch to the back and gently pulling the thread to close the gap. Imagine making a Z shape over the seam. **4**

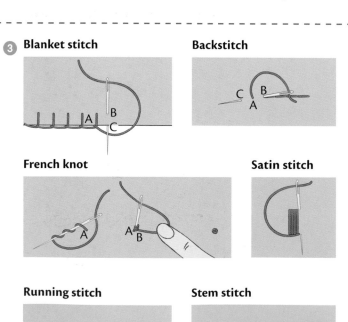

3 **Blanket stitch**

Backstitch

French knot

Satin stitch

Running stitch

Stem stitch

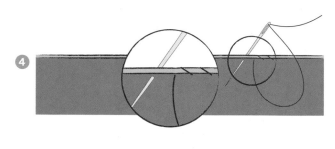

4

3. To finish, make several tiny stitches on top of each other and snip the thread. The smaller and shallower your stitches, the less obvious the seam will be.

Ladder stitch. This stitch makes a great hidden seam, so it's perfect for a seam that will be visible or any outside seam that you can't sew from the inside. It's important to make small ladder stitches, because your seam may start to curve between stitches if they're too long.

1. To start a ladder stitch, anchor your knot on the underside of the seam allowance on one of the fabrics to be joined and bring the needle out through the folded edge. Insert the needle through the fold on the opposite edge and bring it out through the fold about ¼" away.

2. Insert the needle into the opposite fold directly across from where the thread emerged and take a stitch into this fold. Continue in this manner, stitching back and forth across the folds for the length of the opening and gently pulling on the thread as you make each stitch to close the gap. You should begin to see a "ladder" of stitches form. ⑤

3. Anchor your thread at the end with several small stitches on top of each other, and then snip the excess thread.

Blind hem stitch. Use the blind hem stitch to hand stitch bindings to a quilt or any project that has binding.

1. Anchor your thread under the fold of your binding to hide the knot, and then bring the needle up through the front of the binding very near the edge of the fold.

2. Insert the needle into the project backing just above where it came out at the binding. Go one stitch length and come out through the binding near the fold again. Make sure you don't stitch through all the layers—just catch the backing fabric. ⑥

3. Continue, being careful to catch just a few threads of the binding each time (this is what makes it an invisible stitch).

Topstitching. Topstitching shows "on top" of the fabric and functions as a decorative element. Topstitching is pretty self-explanatory, but here are a few tips:

• Use a straight stitch set at a standard short-to-medium length.

• When topstitching around the perimeter of a project or along a pocket fold, sewing ⅛" from the edge is about right. How close is an aesthetic choice, so if you prefer a slightly larger space, topstitch ¼" from the edge.

• Try using one of the inner indentations on your presser foot as a guide. It works not only as a visual guide, but often also helps keep the fabric "in line."

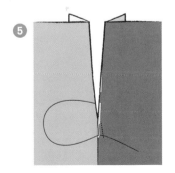
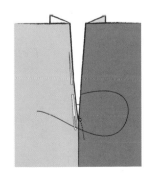
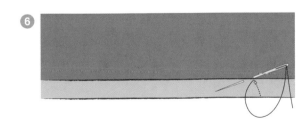

The techniques involved in quiltmaking could fill many books, but we'll cover enough of the basics to get you started.

the quilt sandwich

Once you have a quilt top (or anything that will be layered with batting, like a pot holder), you'll make a "quilt sandwich" of the top, batting, and backing fabric. When preparing the layers, make sure the batting and backing are 4" larger than the top on each edge. (You'll trim the excess before binding the quilt.) Unless you plan to use the piecing seams as quilting guides, mark the quilt top before you make the "sandwich." ①

machine quilting

Quilting can be as simple as a diagonal grid or as complex as large swooping feathers or pictorial designs. If you don't want to take on the challenge of machine quilting your own quilt, hire a professional long-arm quilter. Straight-line quilting is very approachable for any sewist, whereas free-motion quilting requires some practice. If you'd like to give it a shot, make a stack of 12" x 12" quilt sandwiches, lower your feed dogs, and start stitching! Free-motion quilting is like drawing with your machine, except that you move the paper instead of the pencil.

Straight-line machine quilting is easy to do, and using a walking foot makes it as simple as sewing a straight seam.

1. Layer your quilt top with batting and backing. Pin baste with safety pins.

2. Using matching top and bobbin thread, machine stitch along your marked design. At the beginning and end of a stitching line, backstitch or make ¼" of very short stitches.

3. Switch direction often to prevent the quilt from becoming skewed. For example, when quilting a project with a diagonal grid, sew one line from the lower left to the upper right, then stitch the next line from the upper left to the lower right, and so on.

binding

Binding encloses the raw edges of the quilt sandwich. Bindings can be stitched by hand or machine. Hand-stitched bindings are more time-consuming, but they look beautiful. Machine-stitched bindings are a great alternative if you hate hand sewing or are in a rush. Experiment with both and decide which you prefer. Before you begin either method, trim the excess batting and backing.

hand-stitched binding

1. Sew the binding strips end to end to make one long strip; press the seam allowances open. Press the strip in half lengthwise, wrong sides together.

2. Lay the binding flat on the front of the project with the raw edges aligned; pin along one edge. Using a ¼" seam allowance, begin sewing several inches from the end of the binding. Stop stitching ¼" from the corner and backstitch. ②

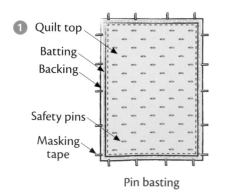

① Quilt top
Batting
Backing

Safety pins

Masking tape

Pin basting

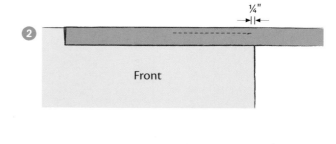

② ¼"

Front

3. Fold the end of the binding up at a 90° angle to make a 45°-angle fold. Then fold the binding straight down, aligning the raw edges of the binding with the raw edges of the next side to be sewn. Start stitching at the fold, backstitch, and continue sewing the binding to that side. Stop sewing ¼" from the corner and repeat the folding technique. Continue around the remaining sides of the project. ③

4. Stop a few inches before your starting point. Lay your two binding tails flat against the quilt edge and overlap them ½"; trim the excess.

5. Open the binding, place the ends right sides together, and join them with a ¼" seam. Finger-press the seam allowance open. ④

6. Refold the binding and finish stitching it to the edge of the project.

7. Fold the binding to the back, just covering the first line of stitching. Use metal hair clips or pins to secure.

8. When you reach a corner, fold over the first side completely, and then fold over the second side to miter the corner. ⑤

9. Refer to "Finishing Stitches" (page 106) and use a blind hem stitch to secure the binding to the quilt back, or refer to "Machine-Stitched Binding" below to stitch it by machine.

machine-stitched binding

Attach the binding to the project as described in steps 1–8 of "Hand-Stitched Binding," except stitch the binding to the *back* of the project and fold it to the front. Secure the binding with straight pins. Using matching top and bobbin thread and your walking foot, topstitch the binding ⅛" from the folded edge. When you reach a corner, insert the needle into the mitered fold, pivot, and continue stitching. Remember to backstitch at the beginning and end.

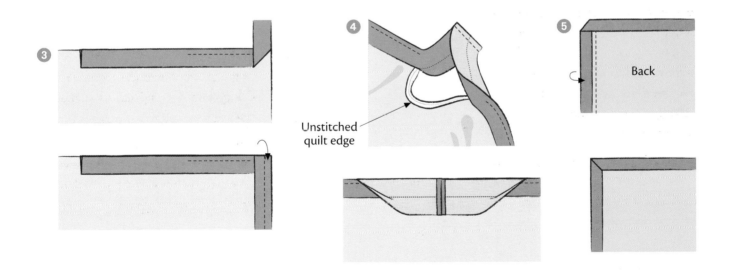

Unstitched quilt edge

Back

online RESOURCES

There are so many wonderful shops and websites that sell fabric and tools from online. There's no way we could list them all, but here are a few of our current favorites.

ETSY
www.etsy.com
An ever-changing selection of designer and Japanese fabrics, felts, notions, and other materials including:

- **LIT'L BROWN BIRD**
  www.etsy.com/shop/Litlbrownbird
  SUN FELT Japanese brand of felt

- **FILZ FELT**
  www.etsy.com/shop/FilzFelt
  100% German wool felt

- **TANTALIZING STITCHES**
  www.etsy.com/shop/tantalizing-stitches
  Bag-making supplies and hardware

FAT QUARTER SHOP
www.fatquartershop.com
Quilting cottons and designer prints

HARTS FABRIC
www.hartsfabric.com
Quilting cottons and a variety of canvas and upholstery-weight fabrics

PURL SOHO
www.purlsoho.com
459 Broome Street
New York, NY 10013
A wide variety of fabric, sewing, and craft supplies

SEATTLE FABRICS
www.seattlefabrics.com
8702 Aurora Avenue N.
Seattle, WA 98103
Ripstop nylon, closed-cell foam, and bag hardware; a great source for all manner of outdoor fabrics

SUPER BUZZY
www.superbuzzy.com
1932 Eastman Avenue #106
Ventura, CA 93003
Japanese fabric and craft supplies

acknowledgments

So many people took part in the making of this book, and we want to take this opportunity to single out a few here:

- To the talented folks at Martingale & Company, thank you for this wonderful opportunity!

- Dawn Anderson and Cathy Valentine for their beautiful machine and hand quilting.

- Freespirit and Moda for generously donating their gorgeous fabrics for us to work with.

- Our neighborhood quilt and fabric shops here in Seattle: The Quilting Loft, Stitches, Pacific Fabrics, Gathering Fabrics, Quiltworks Northwest, and Seattle Fabrics. We're thankful to have such great resources right at our fingertips.

- To all of our friends, family, and coworkers who test-sewed or edited patterns, gave feedback, or provided moral support during this odyssey: we are so lucky to be surrounded by such a creative and supportive community!

about the authors

Cassie Barden has a lifelong history of making art, from cartooning, film making, painting, and digital illustration to making odd stuffed animals and creating costumes for the Burning Man festival. She has sewn off and on most of her life but it wasn't until after college that she started designing her own patterns. She is inspired by contemporary art, design, illustration, technology, and anything handmade. She published her first book, *The New Handmade*, with Martingale & Company in 2008. You can see more of her patterns in *A Baker's Dozen* (2010), *Jelly Babies* (2011), and *Sew the Perfect Gift* (fall 2011), all from Martingale & Company.

Adrienne Smitke grew up surrounded by crafts in a house full of handmade quilts and clothes. Adrienne's mother taught her to sew at an early age, even once assigning sewing "homework" over summer vacation. She made a rad pair of black-and-neon-green shorts. (It was the '80s, after all.) Drawing on her creative childhood, Adrienne studied illustration and graphic design in college, during which she finally began experimenting with sewing again on her own. You can see more of her patterns in *A Baker's Dozen*, *Jelly Babies*, and *Sew the Perfect Gift*, all from Martingale & Company.

Cassie and Adrienne both live in the Ballard neighborhood of Seattle, Washington.

There's More Online!

Visit www.handmadeisawesome.com for video tutorials, free pattern extras, and to share your project photos online!

For more books on sewing and quilting, go to www.martingale-pub.com.

you might also enjoy these other fine titles from
MARTINGALE & COMPANY

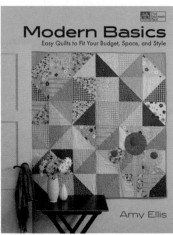
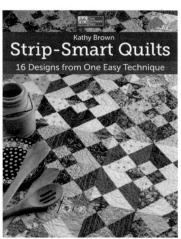

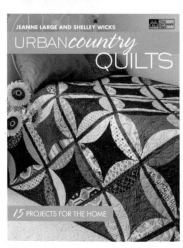